DEATH,
DYNAMITE
AND
DISASTER

T0150416

DEATH, DYNAMITE
AND
DISASTER

A GRISLY BRITISH
RAILWAY HISTORY

ROSA MATHESON

First published 2014
This paperback edition published 2022

The History Press
97 St George's Place, Cheltenham,
Gloucestershire, GL50 3QB
www.thehistorypress.co.uk

British Library Cataloguing in Publication Data.
A catalogue record for this book is available from the British Library.

ISBN 978 0 7509 9894 9

Typesetting and origination by The History Press
Printed and bound in Great Britain by TJ Books Limited, Padstow, Cornwall.

Trees for LYfe

CONTENTS

ACKNOWLEDGEMENTS

Whilst writing this book, I have had the enormous pleasure of 'meeting' (over the internet, email, telephone, or letter) many new people who have been more than kind and helpful to a total stranger. I thank them not just for their support, their genuine interest and enthusiasm, but also for their trust. It is wonderfully reassuring to find such people are around. I have many people to thank, as this book has been something of a team effort – so, a big 'thank you' to – Anna Stone, archivist at Aviva, for searching the archive, sending and reviewing material and the use of graphics; Dave Pennington of the London & North Western Railway Society for digging out articles; Peter Witts of the Midland Railway Society, who went out of his way to find material and helpful sources and look over drafts; Richard Flindell and the archaeologists at Network Rail for passing on the fruits of their work; Dave Chapman for guidance and input on explosives; Paul Hindle of Manchester Geographical Society for pointing me in a good direction; and John Clarke who made time for friendly conversations, direction and support.

Rev. Canon Brian Arman, Ken Gibbs, Jack Hayward, Clive Foxell, and Elaine Chapman, archivist at STEAM Museum, Swindon; Viv Head and Richard Stacpoole-Ryding of the British Transport Police History Group, and Sheffield History Group, all offered advice, suggestions and sources. Chris Heaven gladly sent on a precious book for me to read, as did Hugh Epstein of the Conrad Society; Angela Bell of the Thomas Hardy Society immediately responded with very helpful information; Sue McNaughton of 'Wandleys on the Web' courageously ploughed through her large volumes of *Punch*; and Peter Cross-Rudkin of the Railway & Canal Historical Society (R&CHS) replied with a speed that was outstanding. Thanks, Peter, and the R&CHS for trying to ascertain more information on the 'spear break' (something of a mystery to all), and to Alan M. Levitt, in New York, who responded with a plausible suggestion.

I have been fortunate indeed, with help and advice from those with a passion and knowledge of the mysteries of the Tay Bridge Disaster. Members of three groups need special mention: Donald Cattanach and Allan Rodgers of the North British Railway Study Group; David Swinfen of the Tay Rail Bridge Disaster Memorial Trust and Murray Nicoll of the Tay Valley Family History Society, who all gave immense and valued help. Another, Peter Lewis of the Open University, happily offered and sent his literature. All gave generously of their time, knowledge and expertise, but also kindly shared their findings and research which saved me time and possible mistakes. A memorial to all those known who perished was erected in December 2013 close by the Tay Bridge.

To those who have allowed the use of photographs and images, many thanks. They all add value to the book. A special thank you to those who run historical websites, they have provided a useful starting point and sources. To those who escaped memory, I offer an encompassing 'thanks' and my apologies. I will endeavour to put it right in the next edition.

As always, I thank my family for their continued interest in my railway world, especially my husband, Ian, for his time, his patience, and tolerance of hearing me go on and on about it, and for reading it over.

INTRODUCTION

RAILWAY ACCIDENTS

Death, Dynamite, Disaster – all words that stir the blood as well as the imagination; all words, however, that one would rather not imagine in the context of today's railways or Underground.[1]

Nowadays, railways are accepted as 'commonplace' and travelling on them is an everyday occurrence. We no longer talk of the 'wonder of the railways', if indeed we talk of them at all – we just expect them to be there. We also expect them to be safe. We do not travel anticipating accidents or serious mishap. Neither do we undertake new railway projects expecting that workers will lose their lives or suffer horrendous injury; however, in the early days of the railways – their birth, infancy and toddler years – everything connected to railways: building and working on them; walking by or crossing them; getting into and travelling on them; even waiting patiently at the station was fraught with danger. Indeed, it can be said that death and injury on nineteenth-century British railways occurred so regularly – almost daily in earliest times – as to be regarded as 'commonplace'. So commonplace that railway accidents became part and parcel of modern Victorian life and so familiar that even new medical terms entered the vernacular of railways. So commonplace, in fact, that they offered an entrepreneurial opportunity in the guise of 'The Railway Passengers' Assurance Company'. Whilst 'Life Assurance' had been around for quite some time, assurance for accidents was unheard of.

'The Universal Railway Casualty Compensation Company' was the brainwave of solicitor H.F. Holt after a conversation with his clerk. He declared his intention of creating a company, in November 1848, in an advertisement stating, '... for the purpose of insuring the lives of persons travelling in Great Britain and Ireland, against Accidents on Railways *and* for affording compensation for injuries sustained by such accidents ...'

The company was officially started in December 1848, and was known only for three days under this initial name, thereafter it became 'The Railway Passengers' Assurance Company'. What differentiated this company from other life assurance companies was the '*and*' (my italics, because here is the big difference): 'and to grant in cases of accident not having a fatal termination compensation to the assured for injuries received under certain conditions'; thus 'The Railway Passengers' Assurance Company' was the first of its kind and a true pioneer in the field.

In order for the initiative to be successful, agreement had to be obtained from the railway companies for their booking clerks to sell the insurance for journeys along with the travel tickets. In return for this, the companies would receive commission on the sales, 50 per cent of which would go to the setting up of a Benevolent Fund for railway employees. Agreement had also to be obtained from the Chancellor of the Exchequer to accept a percentage tax on premiums, rather than stamp duty on each policy issued. This was vital to the success of the company, as booking clerks would not have been able to sell the insurance if each policy had needed to be stamped upon purchase. Premiums varied according to the class of travel, since those sitting in the roofless second and exposed third-class coaches were at higher risk than those comfortably ensconced in first class. An advertisement in *The Times*, in January 1849, stated these terms, 'for the sum of 3*d*, a first-class passenger to insure £1,000 in case of death, second class 2*d*, to insure £500; third class 1*d*, to insure £200 and in case of accident only a sum of money to be promptly paid in proportion to the extent of injury sustained.'[2]

The Railway Passengers' Assurance Company could only deliver their product with the co-operation of the individual railway companies. Here we can see that eight have come onboard. What made this insurance so radical was the fact that it was insuring not only for loss of life, but also for injury. (Aviva)

This 'ticket', No. 3264, issued to Mr John Steel at a premium of £1, covered him for £1,000 for loss of life and a proportion of such 'in the event of his sustaining personal injury … whilst travelling in any class Carriage … in Great Britain or Ireland', for one whole year. It makes one think that Mr Steel had occasion to travel by railway a lot. (Aviva)

IMPORTANT TO RAILWAY TRAVELLERS.

RAILWAY PASSENGERS ASSURANCE COMPANY.
EMPOWERED BY SPECIAL ACT OF PARLIAMENT.

Capital, One Million.

Offices, No. 3, Old Broad Street, London.

The Company's Single Journey Tickets are now obtainable on the following Railways :—

> London and North Western,
> Lancashire and Yorkshire,
> Chester and Holyhead,
> Lancaster and Carlisle,
> Caledonian,
> North British,
> Edinburgh and Glasgow, and
> Eastern Counties,

and arrangements for their issue on other lines of Railway will be shortly announced. **THE RATES OF PREMIUM ARE—**

3d.	To insure £1000 to a First-class Passenger.
2d.	"	500 to a Second-class "
1d.	"	200 to a Third-class "

PERIODICAL TICKETS may be obtained at the Company's Offices, 3, Old Broad Street, London ; of the Provincial Agents of the Company ; and the Booking Clerks at all Railway Stations where Single Journey Tickets are issued.

To insure £1,000 for Three Months, at a premium of 10s.
" 1,000 for Six Months, " 16s.
" 1,000 for Twelve Months, " £1.

These Tickets allow the holder the option of travelling in any class carriage, and on any railway in the United Kingdom. The amount will be paid to the representatives of the Assured in the event of a fatal accident ; and in case of personal injury, liberal compensation will be made. The premium charged includes the Stamp Duty.

ALEXANDER BEATTIE, Secretary.

By 1850, it was operating on thirty-two railways and, between January and September of that year, had issued 2,808 periodical tickets and 110,074 single journey tickets. In June 1852, a new act was passed enabling the company to insure any person against any kind of accident, which it employed somewhat later, in September 1855.[3]

The company's first claimant, William Good of Dunstable, made his claim in November 1849, following an accident between Penrith and Preston, and was awarded a generous £7 6s. Other assurance companies were quick to see the potential of such business, seeking to join forces with the RPA Company (with no success), whilst others, like the British Railway Passenger Association (later renamed the Passenger Assurance Company), set up alone.

The RPA Company were quick to send their representatives to the scene of any disaster. Just days after the Tay Bridge accident on Sunday 28 December 1879, the *Aberdeen Journal* reported (on 1 January 1880) that Mr C.H. Dalton, RPA superintendent, had already arrived on the scene to 'communicate without delay with the relatives of any passengers ... who may have been in possession of the company's tickets or policies.' It found that one victim, W.H. Beynon, 'held a policy against accidents of all kinds for £1000'.[4] In its early years, the RPA Company dispatched a surgeon to each accident scene to see that the insured received proper attention, and that their claims were settled as speedily as possible. It was also not unknown for the company to advance money to a claimant to go for

HOW TO INSURE AGAINST RAILWAY ACCIDENTS.
TIE A COUPLE OF DIRECTORS À LA MAZEPPA TO EVERY ENGINE THAT STARTS WITH A TRAIN.

Such were the numbers and regularity of railway accidents that there was a great deal of hostility towards directors of railway companies, as this cartoon shows.

convalescence, in order to regain their strength before making their claim – service indeed!

The Railway Passengers' Assurance Company weathered some rocky moments in its long history, up until 2005 when it was dissolved and its business absorbed into that of Commercial Union, which is now part of Aviva.

The reputation of railway companies in connection with accidents was dismal, even though some, like contemporary railway writer Samuel Smiles, argued how safe the railways were:

> The remarkable safety with which railway traffic is on the whole conducted, is due to constant watchfulness and highly-applied skill. The men who work the railways are for the most part the picked men of the country, and every railway station may be regarded as a practical school of industry, attention, and punctuality. Where railways fail in these respects, it will usually be found that it is because the men are personally defective, or because better men are not to be had. It must also be added that the onerous and responsible duties which railway workmen are called upon to perform require a degree of consideration on the part of the public which is not very often extended to them.[5]

The statistics from the Returns to the Railway Department of the Board of Trade – such as this one, ending June 1887 (written up by *Illustrated London News*) – give different insight:

> There were reported eighteen collisions between passenger-trains by which sixty-four passengers and nine railway servants were injured; twelve collisions between passenger-trains and goods or mineral trains, by which seventy-six passengers and twelve servants were injured; seven collisions between goods-trains, by which two servants were killed and fifteen persons injured; twenty cases of passenger-trains leaving the rails, by which one servant was killed and eighteen persons injured; four cases of goods-trains leaving the rails, by which three servants were killed; and ten cases of trains running into stations or sidings at too high speed, by which twenty passengers and two railway servants were injured.[6]

And another report, five years later for the six-month period ending June 1892, written up in the *Great Western Railway Magazine*, listed 381 accidents of various kinds: collisions between passenger trains; collision between passenger and goods or mineral trains; passenger trains leaving the rails; trains or engines travelling in the wrong direction through points; trains running into stations at high speed; failures of axles, couplings, a bridge and the rails themselves – all resulting in eleven passengers and three railway servants killed and 282 passengers and thirty-two servants injured.[7] These, along with the numerous articles and editorials in the national, local and railway papers, over decades of time, show that associating with the railways was undoubtedly a hazardous affair. In his book *Railway Accidents – Legislation and Statistics 1825–1924*, full of meticulously detailed facts, numbers and statistics, Raynar H. Wilson states that, between 1871 and 1890 (inclusive), there were 2,473 accidents of various classes and enough seriousness to warrant being inquired into.

Accidents from crossing the rails, whether at level crossings or in stations, were notorious. The numbers of deaths each year were horrific, and time and again the matter was raised in Parliament. Mr Channing, MP (Northampton, E.), addressed the House of Commons regarding what he dryly called, 'this most fruitful source of accidents!'[8] He quoted figures from the Returns of 1885 and 1886, stating that, in 1885, there were ninety-three persons killed and thirty-four persons injured at level crossings, and in 1886 there were 104 killed and fifty-two persons injured (that is more than two killed and one injured in every week of the year).[9]

Even in the closing decade of the century, such accidents were so commonplace that they were often not reported in newspapers under straplines connecting it to the railway; rather, something 'other' was used in order to capture the reader's attention, such as 'COMMERCIAL TRAVELLER KILLED'. In this instance, the report is on the 'terrible accident' of a 'well-dressed gentleman'; a commercial traveller called Firth, who made his way to the Midland Railway's King's Heath Station after a hard day's work calling on local tradesmen. The layout of the station meant that he had to 'cross the rails' and, whilst doing so, he slipped and fell in front of the 6.25 p.m. train from King's Norton.

To the horror of the driver and others present 'the engine passed over the middle of his body and completely severed it'.[10]

Railway accidents impacted hugely on a Victorian society trying to get to grips with the new world of industrialisation, science and technology; a fast-moving and rapidly changing world, one with a constant shifting in society's values and culture. It was a challenging and exciting time, but full of tensions and anxieties brought about by having to deal with the unknown, and railway accidents became the physical manifestation of collective anxieties. From the very beginning of the railway age the number and nature of railway accidents was truly shocking, as was the number and nature of deaths and injuries. For the travelling public, what was especially worrisome about railway accidents was not just what happened to one at the time of the incident, but what could later happen as a result of it — one could become seriously ill and disabled by 'shock' itself. For a society traumatized by such events, the railway accident became an iconic symbol of the nation's shock. Dr Furneaux Jordan, an eminent physician of the time, wrote in 1882:

> All that the most powerful impression on the nervous system can effect, is effected in a railway accident … The incidents of a railway accident contribute to form a combination of the most terrible circumstances which it is possible for the mind to conceive. The vastness of the destructive forces, the magnitude of the results, the imminent danger to the lives of numbers of human beings and the hopelessness of escape of the danger, give rise to emotion which in themselves are quite sufficient to produce shock, or even death itself.[11]

Inspecting Officers of the Railway Department of the Board of Trade played a large part in the investigation of railway accidents. Recruited from the Corps of Royal Engineers, they brought a wealth of technical knowledge, experience and a professional integrity to their new roles. The Railway Inspectorate, under the umbrella of the Board of Trade, came into being in 1840 as a result of the Railway Regulations Act (1840). The inspectors were experienced engineers, but were recruited purely from the military. Their job was to investigate accidents reported by railway companies to the Board of Trade, and thence to report their findings to Parliament. These reports were published and made available to everyone – including the public. The Inspectorate was also tasked with inspecting new lines, and commenting on their suitability for carrying passenger traffic.

The Inspectorate's first investigation, carried out by General Sir John Mark Frederick Smith, the first head of the Inspectorate, concerned the Howden accident on 7 August 1840. A Hull & Selby passenger train was travelling from Leeds to Hull when a large casting from a weighing machine fell from a wagon just behind the tender, causing a derailment of the following passenger carriages. The first five carriages were luckily empty, but the sixth held several passengers, four of whom were killed. After conducting a thorough investigation, and determining that the machine had been unsecured and overhanging the sides of the wagon, Smith's recommendations were that goods should only be carried when they were secured, and that all wagons should be fitted with a frame to prevent items falling off; however, herein was the weakness of the Inspectorate, because despite being able to lawfully prohibit the opening and operation of any new railway unless it met all the regulations laid down by the government, they had no powers to enforce their recommendations in respect of accidents on existing railways. It was to prove a great frustration to them. Relationships between railway companies and the Inspectorate were another problem. They were never of the most cordial, much antagonism emanating from the railways who resented being inspected and reported upon by 'military men' rather than 'railway men'. In its very first issue, in 1897, *The Railway Magazine* (a very pro-railway companies production) took up its cudgels on behalf of the companies, suggesting of the inspectors, 'It's not so much wot 'e sees, but the nasty way he sees it.'[12]

Sometimes, the accidents investigated by the Inspectorate were found to be the result of mischievousness or even malice; however, at the time of its inauguration, few, if any, would have thought of the railways being under sustained and deliberate attack for political reasons but, during the 'dynamite decades' of the 1880s and 1890s, this was to be the case. A different organisation became involved in such incidents – the Home Office Explosives Department – to counter Britain's first wave of terrorism.

DEATH

THE MELANCHOLY DEATH OF THE UNFORTUNATE MR HUSKISSON

The opening of the Liverpool & Manchester Railway was a momentous day. Indeed, it was a day that changed the world, as it heralded the 'Age of the Railways'. At the opening of this 'great national work'[1] on the morning of 15 September 1830, the scene at Liverpool's Edge Hill Station was one of colour, festivity and triumph. 'The numbers congregated were immense and popular expectation was excited to the highest degree', stated the *Guardian*, some three days later. Indeed, Liverpool was full to bursting, so eager were the people of the nation to witness this great event. 'Never was there such an assemblage of rank, wealth, beauty and fashion, in this neighbourhood.'[2] The *Staffordshire Advertiser* reported, 'It was computed that not less than 500,000 persons were assembled throughout the whole line.'[3] 'A Railer',[4] an invited guest, writing in *Blackwood's Edinburgh Magazine*, captures that breathless and unbelieving atmosphere:

> There was a feverish conspiracy of pleasure, of curiosity, and perhaps, beyond what many chose to express or encourage, of solemn forebodings, of secret presentiments, of those qualms and misgivings of all sorts and sizes, which are wont to haunt timid minds when placed in situations to which they are unused.[5]

Whilst another guest passenger, Fanny Kemble, famous and popular actress of the period, author and anti-slavery campaigner, recalls, 'The most intense curiosity and excitement prevailed, and though the weather was uncertain enormous masses of densely packed people lined the road, shouting and waving hats and handkerchiefs.'

It had not always been thus. The coming of the railway and the huge high-wheeled steam 'monsters' had not been to everyone's liking. Large numbers of the population were against it and afraid of it for many reasons. Canal owners and boatmen feared for their livelihoods, as did coachmen and the owners of the horse-drawn stage coaches. Country folk were worried for the welfare of their livestock when the trains roared past spouting smoke and fire. Would the animals drop dead with fright? Would the cows' milk dry up? Would the cinders set fire to the land?

Many, scientists and physicians amongst them, were worried for the people's health; could they cope with such noise, and travel at such speeds? Would they lose their senses? Would they become physically impaired or even 'done to death' by such an experience? Such was the consternation that, as they worked to lay the 31 miles of track between the first ever intercity termini in Liverpool (Crown Street) and Manchester (Liverpool Road/Water Street), the workmen – the navvies – were abused verbally, and even physically, with bricks and stones. It is said that the company secretary slept with a gun on his bedside table.[6]

Little wonder then, at the relief, the joy and celebration of this wondrous and hard-fought outcome of man's scientific (and political) endeavours. Such an occasion demanded all the pomp and ceremony, splendour and élan the directors of this new, prestigious railway company could muster, and they proudly rose to the occasion. They were determined to get things right, and planned the event with military precision. They put together an 'Orders of the Day' to inform guests what would happen, what to do and when to do it, so that all would run smoothly and without incident. Just as importantly, they also informed the travellers of what not to do, and it was the disregard for the latter that caused a great tragedy and changed 'a scene of gaiety and splendour into one of horror and dismay'.[7]

ORDERS OF THE DAY

LIVERPOOL SEPTEMBER 15TH 1830

The Directors will meet at the Station, in Crown Street, not later than Nine o'clock in the Morning, and during the assembling of the Company, will severally take charge of separate Trains of Carriages to be drawn by different Engines as follows:

NORTHUMBRIAN	*Lilac Flag*
PHOENIX	*Green Flag*
NORTH STAR	*Yellow Flag*
ROCKET	*Light Blue Flag*
DART	*Purple Flag*
COMET	*Deep Red Flag*
ARROW	*Pink Flag*
METEOR	*Brown Flag*

The men who have the management of the Carriage-breaks will be distinguished by a white ribbon round the arm.

When the Train of Carriage are attached to their respective Engines a Gun will be fired as a preliminary signal, when the "Northumbrian" will take her place at the

Head of the Procession; a second Gun will be fired, and the whole will move forward.

The Engines will stop at Parkside (a little beyond Newton) to take in a supply of water, *during which the Company are requested not to leave their Carriage.*[8]

At Manchester the Company will alight and remain one hour to partake of the Refreshments which will be provided in the Warehouses at that station. In the Furthest warehouse on the right hand side will be the Ladies' Cloak Room.

Before Leaving the Refreshment Rooms a Blue Flag will be exhibited as a signal for the Ladies to resume their Cloaks; after which the Company will repair to their respective Carriages, which will be ranged in the same order as before and sufficient time will be allowed for everyone to take his seat, according to the number of his

Ticket, in the Train to which he belongs; and Ladies and Gentlemen
are particularly requested not to part with their Tickets during the
day, as it is by the number and colour of the Tickets that they will
be enabled at all times to find with facility their respective places in
the Procession.

To help celebrate this memorable occasion, the 'great' and the 'good'
of the land had all been invited − the Prime Minister (the Duke
of Wellington), Mr Home Secretary (Sir Robert Peel), a Prince, a
Marquis, Viscounts, Earls, Dukes and Lords and Ladies, as well as a
Count, an Admiral and a Bishop, many 'Sirs', Ambassadors, VIP dignitaries, business men of repute[9] and those in the 'fashionable' echelons
of Society, such as the aforementioned actress, Fanny Kemble. There
were, perhaps ironically, also three medical persons amongst the
guests − Mr Joseph P. Brandreth, a surgeon of Liverpool, Mr Hunter,
a surgeon of Edinburgh Hospital, and Dr Southey, of London, (all of
whom, according to Brandreth, were later to play a significant role in
the unfolding drama).[10]

The Right Honourable William Huskisson, MP (11 March 1770–
15 September 1830), a director of the Liverpool & Manchester
Railway Company, was, at the time of his death, the locally popular
Liberal representative for Liverpool. He was an active leader in the
movement towards Free Trade; and had been the President of the
Board of Trade from 1822–28. It was whilst he was in this post

The opening of
the Liverpool
& Manchester
Railway was
a lavish affair
when the 'great'
and the 'good'
gathered together
to celebrate and
wonder at the
marvels of science
and men's genius.

that he offered to resign, when the House of Lords failed to pass a bill to give Manchester its own Member of Parliament. Wellington called Huskisson's bluff by accepting his resignation. Huskisson had been publicly humiliated, and relations between the two men were cool and distant thereafter. Charles Greville, a respected and well-placed contemporary diarist of the time, wrote of Huskisson:

> There is no man in Parliament, or perhaps out of it, so well versed in finance, commerce, trade and colonial matters ... As a speaker in the House of Commons he was luminous upon his own subject, but he had no pretensions to eloquence; his voice was feeble, and his manner ungraceful ... In society he was extremely agreeable, without much animation, generally cheerful, with a great deal of humour, information, and anecdote, gentlemanlike, unassuming, slow in speech, and with a down-cast look, as if he avoided meeting anybody's gaze. [11]

Greville described Huskisson as, 'about sixty years old, tall, slouching, and ignoble-looking', and remarks on his 'peculiar aptitude for accidents', whilst Simon Garfield indicates that Huskisson was a permanent 'accident waiting to happen'. He cites him falling from his horse, his carriage and even from his bed! Significantly, Huskisson had 'dislocated his ankle in 1801 and was in consequence slightly lame' and had also 'fractured his arm three times, the last time leaving him slightly impaired'. [12] Everyone knew that Huskisson had been in ill-health for some time and, at the Opening, was still suffering from the consequences of having to attend the lengthy funeral service for King George IV in June. Thomas Creevey wrote to a friend following the accident:

> Calcraft tells me that Huskisson's long confinement in St George's Chapel at the King's funeral brought on a complaint ... that made some severe surgical operation necessary, the effect of which had been, according to what he told Calcraft, to paralyse, as it were one leg and thigh, which no doubt, must have increased, if it did not create, his danger and [caused him to] lose his life. [13]

He goes on to remark that Huskisson's arrival 'was unexpected', as he had actually written to say 'his health would not let him come'. Garfield, however, also believes that, on the fateful day, Huskisson was not just in 'poor health' but that he was not as bright and perky as he should have been, being 'slowed-down' and 'hung-over' from an over-enthusiastic 'Eve-of-Launch' party.

The cortège of trains was assembled and ready to carry the passengers – around 600 persons. The eight locomotive engines, had all been constructed at the Stephenson works, and all, undoubtedly, tried and tested to ensure maximum and smooth performance on the great day. From Samuel Smiles, we learn who had the particular honour of driving these impressive 'mechanical beasts' on this special day. He writes:

> The 'Northumbrian' engine, driven by George Stephenson himself, headed the line of trains; then followed the 'Phoenix', driven by Robert Stephenson; the 'North Star', by Robert Stephenson senior (brother of George); the 'Rocket', by Joseph Locke; the 'Dart', by Thomas L. Gooch; the 'Comet', by William Allcard; the 'Arrow', by Frederick Swanwick and the 'Meteor', by Anthony Harding. [14]

The names of these men, and the names of their engines, would not only become household names of their time but were destined to become part of the fabric of British railway history.

The Duke of Wellington (known to have little love for the railways), Sir Robert Peel, Huskisson, and a number of other distinguished persons, were to travel with the directors at the head of the cortège. They rode in a 'truly magnificent carriage' with finely decorated ornamental sides, and a 24ft long canopy mounted on gilded pillars with rich crimson drapery, and 'the whole surmounted by the ducal crown', constructed so that it could be lowered for the tunnels. There was a central ottoman for seating, and the whole 32ft long by 8ft wide carriage was carried on eight gigantic 'large iron wheels'. [15] Huskisson, and other VIPs, were in a carriage on one side of the Duke, with a band of musicians in a carriage on the other, all hauled by the 14 horsepower *Northumbrian* on the south line.

Being the sole train on this line (the L&M Railway was the first twin-tracked railway) ensured that the Prime Minister would not be delayed or entrapped should any other train break down. The remaining trains would travel in order on the northern line: *Phoenix* with five carriages, *North Star* with five carriages, *Rocket* with three carriages, *Dart* with four carriages, *Comet* with four carriages, *Arrow* with four carriages, and *Meteor* with four carriages. The Duke's train would 'lead the way' and then allow the other trains to catch up and, at times, overhaul him. So was the plan. It took some time to muster but, when the Duke finally entered his carriage, a single gun was fired, and all was set in motion. Shortly before 11 a.m. the entourage got underway, slowly at first, rolling downhill to the tunnel at Edge Hill, but soon they were travelling under their own steam 'swifter than a bird flies'.[16]

The opening of the Liverpool & Manchester Railway was a day of many 'firsts'. Not too long after setting out, some 13 miles (21km) out of Liverpool, quite near to Parr, the first collision occurred between passenger trains – a rear-end shunt. 'A Railer' recorded it in detail:

> One of our engine's [the *Phoenix*] wheels, how I know not, contrived to bolt from the course – in plain words, it escaped from the rail, and ploughed along upon the clay, with no other inconvenience than an increase of friction, which damped our speed, and with the additional application of the break, soon brought us to an anchor. The engine, however, behind us, not being aware of our mishap, came pelting on at a smart pace, without receiving its signal for checking motion in time. Accordingly, those on the look-out hastily called on their fellow-passengers to be on their guard, and prepare for a jolt, which took place with a crash upon our rear, sufficiently loud and forcible to give an idea of what would happen, if by any strange chance it had charged us with the unrestrained impetuosity of its powers.

Those who looked for harbingers of doom could be forgiven for thinking that this was one such; however, the engine was soon righted on the rails, and with no casualties, the journey continued.

Parkside Station was located in an isolated rural area (17 miles (27 km) from Liverpool), but it had been designed for future expectations, and built as a water stop and junction station for proposed connections with the Wigan Branch Railway and the Bolton & Leigh Railway, so it already had multiple lines of rails in place. A leaflet, given to those travelling on the trains, explained this and advised that:

> The apparatus at which the water is supplied is worth looking at ... we recommend the inspection to take place from the carriages There are here five lines of rails, and *the excitation arising from the approach of a carriage will generally so confuse a person not accustomed to walk on the railroad, as to make it almost impossible for him to discern which line it is coming on.* [17]

Unhappily, this advice went unheeded. This was the only scheduled stop en route and, by the time they had reached there, the passengers had been travelling just under an hour. Many, some fifty men it is quoted, despite the slight drizzle, felt in need of a 'stretch' and, no doubt, a chance to chat about this wonderful phenomenon. Huskisson, at the suggestion of William Holmes, MP, that it may be a good time to effect a reconciliation with the Duke, approached the Duke's carriage and offered his hand. It is said the two men shook hands 'warmly'. What happened next has become an iconic moment in railway history, often wrongly written up as the 'first death' on the railways.

With so many present, there are several eyewitness accounts to this infamous event, which are recorded and reported with various interpretations. One is from Lady Wilton, who was travelling in the same carriage as the Duke of Wellington and, therefore, close to the point of action. She later graphically told Fanny Kemble what she thought had happened:

> The engine had stopped to take a supply of water, and several of the gentlemen in the directors' carriage had jumped out to look about them. Lord Wilton, Count Batthyany, Count Matuscenitz and Mr Huskisson among the rest were standing talking in the middle of the road, when an engine on the other line, which was parading

up and down merely to show its speed, was seen coming down upon them like lightening. The most active of those in peril sprang back into their seats; Lord Wilton saved his life only by rushing behind the Duke's carriage, and Count Matuscenitz had but just leaped into it, with the engine all but touching his heels as he did so; while poor Mr Huskisson, less active from the effects of age and ill-health, bewildered, too, by the frantic cries of 'Stop the engine! Clear the track!' that resounded on all sides, completely lost his head, looked helplessly to the right and left, and was instantaneously prostrated by the fatal machine, which dashed down like a thunderbolt upon him, and passed over his leg, smashing and mangling it in the most horrible way.

The 'fatal machine' was the engine *Rocket*, under the control of the unfortunate Joseph Locke. Although the winner of the Rainhill Trials – a test for speed and reliability – it was an engine with no brakes. In order to stop, its reverse gear had to be engaged, a practice that took time to accomplish, and on this occasion there was not enough time. It bore down upon the hapless man, knocking him from his tentative hold on the carriage door to the ground, where he landed with his leg bent over the rail – the engine wheel ran over it.

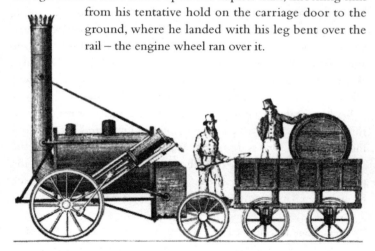

Stephenson's 0-2-2 steam locomotive, *Rocket*, was built in 1829. It gained fame, and its owners' fortune, when it won the Rainhill Trials showing unsurpassed speed and reliability. It gained notoriety when it mowed down the unfortunate Mr Huskisson, causing his death.

Yet another eyewitness, 'A Railer', who was perhaps more professionally detached, writes:

> On looking out, I observed the Duke's train drawn up parallel to another train, with a considerable number of persons on foot assembled in the intervening space; and, at the same time, I perceived an appearance of hustling, and stooping, and crowding together for which I could not well account. In another moment, a gentleman rushed forth, and came running up the line towards us; as he neared, I saw evidently that he was much agitated, and pale and breathless – in short, that something dreadful had happened was obvious. At length he stopped, and fifty voices exclaimed 'Has any thing happened? What is the matter?' In a state of distracted nervousness, and in broken, unconnected words, he at last broke silence – 'Oh God! He is dead! He is killed! He is killed!' – 'Who – and when – and how?' burst from every mouth; the first passing thought on my own, and probably every other mind, being, that some desperate and successful attempt had been made on the Duke's life. The truth, however, soon spread like wildfire to the right and left, acting, as it fell upon every ear, like a spell. Smiles and cheerful countenances were changed for one general gloom. Amongst those who were near the fatal spot, the first feeling was one of thankfulness, that their own immediate relative was not the victim; the next, and most permanent, was sympathy with the unhappy lady who saw her husband stretched, lacerated and bleeding, on the ground.

How could this have happened? Who could have imagined anything like this occurring? Well, those who planned the day had obviously had some thoughts about the possibility of an accident and, in modern terminology, had done a 'health and safety risk assessment', which is why they issued their safety warnings about the 'do's' and the 'don'ts'. Now, despite their best efforts, what they had hoped to prevent had occurred, and in the midst of what had been triumphant celebration and a possible reconciliation between two important men, catastrophe had struck. Where there had been jubilation, now there was shock and horror as news of the human tragedy spread.

Huskisson had fallen on the wet, muddy ground amongst the puddles. He was placed on a door as a makeshift stretcher, dirty and bleeding. He said little apart from asking for his wife, and the words he muttered as others sought to help him were to prove prophetic – 'I have met my death'. An improvised tourniquet, of handkerchiefs and a walking stick, was applied to his injured leg. He was raised up and placed in the carriage behind the *Northumbrian* engine, previously occupied by the band, who were now left to their own devices. Carrying also Huskisson's wife, Lord Wilton, and the three doctors, the train departed for Manchester. The surgeon, Joseph Brandreth, later wrote in some detail about the whole experience. Worried about Huskisson's capacity to make it so far they decided to stop at the nearest accommodation, which was a vicarage near Eccles, the home of Huskisson's friend. They travelled in the open carriage in the wind and rain, although a makeshift screen was erected to try to protect him, and arrived in a 'violent thunder and hail storm'. With great difficulty, they made their way through the barricades of the railway line up to the road, just a few hundred yards from the house. The train continued on to fetch 'surgical aid'. Brandreth administered wine and brandy as they waited for an hour and a half for help and suitable equipment to arrive. With the help of Dr Hunter, he cut the boot and clothes off the injured leg and prepared for an operation should it be 'desired'. He describes the injury and his puzzlement as to how it occurred:

> The leg presented a frightful injury …The leg half way between the knee and ankle was almost entirely severed, except a small portion on the outside, but the boot was scarcely marked at all. Half way but rather higher up between the knee and the body the whole flesh was torn off above the broken bones.
>
> … It is a perfect mystery how the wound was produced … It was scarcely possible to understand how this could take place if the wheel had gone over him, or how only one wheel, and that the first of the engines, could have done so without the whole train following, or why it did not, from the enormous weight, entirely sever it.[18]

Once the equipment and other surgeons had arrived and assessed the situation, it was finally agreed that, because of his condition (his body being shaken regularly by severe spasms), they could not operate and, eventually, they concluded an operation would do nothing to save the poor man. He was administered laudanum, to sedate him and stop the dreadful spasms. (The management and treatment of Huskisson were latterly bitterly contended, the argument being that, if the medical attendees had acted more decisively sooner, his life could have been saved.)

The large, unhappy and shocked party left at the trackside were placed in a quandary – should they go on, or go back? Would it appear unseemly and disrespectful to continue, or if they went back, would the bad news get out, be misrepresented and give the wrong and unhelpful impression of railway travel? Riders on horseback brought news that the large crowds, already gathered at Manchester to see the arrival of the trains and the Duke's party, were growing restless and unhappy in the worsening weather conditions. In order to prevent a possible riot, it was decided to travel on. The remains of the Duke's train was attached to the coupled *Phoenix* and *North Star* trains, and the sorry procession continued its sad, and now uncomfortable journey. On the way they met with George Stephenson, returning from Manchester. Despite the horror of the situation, history was still in the making and another 'first' achieved, as the *Northumbrian*, driven by George Stephenson, is recorded to have made the distance of some 15 miles to the parsonage in Eccles in just twenty-five minutes at a, then mind-blowing, rate of approximately 36mph.

Travelling on through the inclement weather, with buglers no longer playing and passengers no longer responding to the cheering crowds along the route, the bedraggled entourage pulled into Manchester at 3 p.m. Here the crowd, already hostile towards the unpopular Prime Minister and 'the wealthy', had become increasingly restless and agitated. The Duke's carriage, and others, were pelted with vegetables, insults and even stone, as noted later by the *Morning Post*. There were shouts and calls for 'No Corn Laws!' and 'Vote by ballot!'– two very hot and controversial issues on Wellington's political agenda. Fanny Kemble wryly remarked, 'The contrast between our departure from Liverpool and our arrival in Manchester was one of the most striking things I have ever witnessed.'

The military were on hand to greet the Duke (and to protect him and the railway). Wellington cautiously remained in his carriage, talking with well-wishers until he was able to make an early escape, and his train, now pulled by *Comet*, left for the return journey at 4.37 p.m. The rest of the 600 passengers had to wait until the remaining carriages could be gathered and joined together. Then, hauled by the three remaining serviceable engines, they travelled as one long, very slow train, in the darkness, on the home journey to Liverpool, not arriving until after 10 p.m. by which time William Huskisson, MP for Liverpool, was dead.

Whilst his poor wife had found the dreadful situation too much to bear and had to be quieted with sedation, Huskisson showed considerable forbearance and fortitude during his last painful hours, speaking kindly to those who attended him, and even making a codicil to his will and taking holy rites from his friend, the Reverend Blackburn, who had ridden on horseback from Manchester to attend him. He 'breathed his last at 9 o'clock' according to William Wainwright, writing to inform the Mayor of Liverpool; and thereby Huskisson claimed his place in railway history. He was buried with full public ceremonial in Liverpool on the 24 September.

The Right Honourable William Huskisson MP. On his plaque – 'A tribute of personal respect and affection' – it tells how his death 'Changed a moment of the noblest exultation and triumph that science and genius had ever achieved into one of desolation and mourning …'

So popular had he been that 3,000 tickets were issued for his burial in St James' Cemetery, and it is said that almost half the city – some 69,000 – lined the streets to watch the funeral procession and pay their respects. A subscription was set up and, later, a memorial with statue was erected from the monies raised.

Whilst the tragedy reinforced the views of those, like Henry Brougham, who believed the venture to be utterly insane – 'the folly of 700 people going fifteen miles an hour, in six carriages on a narrow road, exceeds belief'[19] – the accident had brought massive media attention. Perhaps ironically, this highlighted the worth of the railway in carrying large numbers and the value of its speed. Whilst further planned celebrations were cancelled, the next day it was 'business as usual' for the Liverpool & Manchester Railway – 'On the following morning the railway was opened for public traffic. The first train of 140 passengers was booked and sent on to Manchester, reaching it in the allotted time of two hours; and from that time the traffic has regularly proceeded from day to day until now.'[20]

The Liverpool & Manchester Railway became an instant success. Writing a perspective on the Liverpool & Manchester Railway, Henry Booth, who had been intimately involved with it, summed up its greatest effect:

> Perhaps the most striking result produced by the completion of this railway, is the sudden and marvellous change which has been effected in our ideas of time and space … what was quick is now slow; what was distant is now near.[21]

George Stephenson learnt lessons from the accident, and had all his new engines equipped with brakes. Wellington remained bitterly opposed to the railways, and did not ride one again until he accompanied Queen Victoria (also known for her lack of love for railways) in 1843, on the London & South Western Railway. William Huskisson's name has become part of our railway heritage. A plaque, marking the spot, commemorates him and his extraordinary passing.

THE ACCIDENT AT SONNING CUTTING – A MERE 'SLIP'!

When Isambard Kingdom Brunel originally planned the Great Western Railway (GWR) line from Bristol to London, he had intended to route the line to the north of Sonning Hill in Berkshire and bypass Sonning village. There was heated objection to this by the local people. In the original act it was proposed to 'pierce the hill by means of a tunnel however the GWR were able to dispense with this and instead a "cutting" which divide[d] the variegated sands and marles of the plastic clay, and passe[d] nearly, but not quite, down to the chalk'[1] was carved through the hill itself.

The cutting, nearly 2 miles long and varying from 20–60ft deep, was an incredible feat of 'man and muscle' as it was dug out by hand and the spoil, around 24,500 cubic yards per week, was removed by wheelbarrow and horse-drawn carts. The amount of excavation necessary was exacerbated by the requirements of the broad gauge rail (7ft ¼in). 'The cross-section of the deepest part of the cutting allowed a width of 30 feet for the railway and 10 feet for the side drains.'[2] It was a massive undertaking and took a back-breaking two years to complete, with many 'navvies' losing their lives in the process. The end result was visually stunning, with the embankment sides rising at an acute angle high above the track. The cutting is traversed by two bridges, which quickly became popular spots for artists and, later, photographers. There are many dramatic presentations of it

J.C. Bourne wrote of this work, 'At its deepest part this cutting is crossed by two bridges. That to the east, represented in the foreground of the accompanying plate, carries the cross road from Sonning towards the Lodden Bridge … the other bridge, also represented in the plate carries the Great Western Turnpike road from London towards Reading.' It would lead one to think that one would be looking at this with one's back to Paddington. It would also suggest that this wooden bridge was the one spoken of in the evidence.

highlighting particular engines and trains as they passed through, especially that of the last broad gauge passenger train behind the engine *Bulkeley* on 20 May 1892.

The view from the old timber bridge in the east was to play a significant role in the following event. On Friday 24 December 1841, the 2-4-0 broad gauge tender engine *Hecla* – one of the GWR's first batch of 'Leo' class engines, designed by Sir Daniel Gooch and built by Fenton, Murray & Jackson of Leeds – left Paddington Station at its usual time of 4.30 a.m. It was hauling a luggage ('goods') train with passengers. (The name of the type of train is of significance here, as it gives an indication of where the priority lay – i.e. luggage/goods over passengers – which was to become a mainstream debate as a result of this event.) In an 1841 timetable, the GWR actually specified that, 'the goods train passengers will be conveyed in uncovered trucks by the goods trains only',[3] in other words, there was no choice of train for them.

The train comprised the engine and tender, two passenger trucks – also known as 'common waggons' (one a six-wheeler and one a four), a truck, and seventeen luggage wagons. The passengers' trucks were placed immediately behind the tender, and herein lay the debate. 'The train was a particularly heavy one being loaded with Christmas cheer, containing amongst other items 800 barrels of oysters and baskets of fish.'[4] The number of passengers reported to have been carried varies between twenty-seven and thirty-eight, but it is agreed that they were chiefly of the 'poorer classes' going home for Christmas.

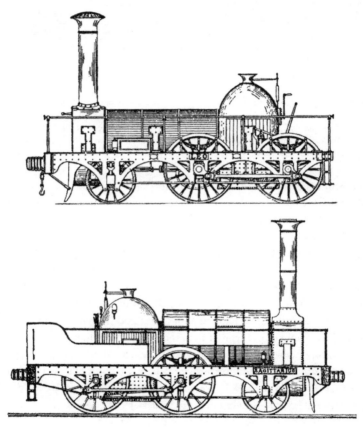

The *Hecla* was one of the Leo class engines designed by Sir Daniel Gooch, and built between January 1841 and July 1842 by three different companies. They were the Great Western Railway's first 'goods' engines. The *Hecla* was built by Fenton, Murray and Jackson of Leeds, whilst these two examples, *Leo* and *Sagittarius*, were built by Rothwell & Co., of Bolton.

It was a dark, gloomy morning; not surprising considering the time of day and time of year. All went as it should until arriving at the Sonning Hill cutting, some 3 miles from Reading, at a place called 'the Gullet' about 80 yards east of the wooden bridge. Due to the recent wet weather conditions, the ground of the great embankment had become saturated, and just before, or maybe even as, the train came through, a slippage of earth occurred, covering the track for about 30 yards and up to 4ft deep.

What happened next was to be written up as 'the first bad Great Western accident' by GWR historian E.T. MacDermott[5] and, perhaps more appropriately, by *The Times* as, 'An accident attended with more deplorable consequences than any that we have yet occasion to record … a most dreadful sacrifice of human life'.[6]

It was the most fatal accident in railway history thus far. So outraged were the public by this latest in a long line of accidents that many sectors of the press joined in the attack on railway companies in general. The *Mechanics' Magazine,* who purported to be 'a serious journal … devoted to scientific accuracy'[7] reported angrily that, 'The railway system has been productive of another appalling accident, the most deplorable, by far … Eight persons in an instant dashed to atoms and twice as many grievously wounded.'[8]

When the engine came into contact with the mass of earth it was immediately forced off the track and onto the side, dragging the tender and most of the train after it. The engine remained upright. The 'next truck which contained the passengers was thrown athwart the lines and in an instant was overwhelmed by the trucks behind which were tossed up in the air by the violence of the collision and fell with fearful force upon it'.[9] It was, reported the *Bristol Mercury,* 'a scene of destruction and horror of the most lamentable and heart-rending character' and *The Times* quoted one eyewitness as saying, 'the scene was horrible in the extreme'.

Miraculously, neither the driver nor the fireman sustained any injury; 'the conductor was thrown from his seat over the bank with great violence but was unhurt as was the guard … other officers of the company were saved by leaping from their places'. The papers praised the driver stating, 'Much credit is due to the engineer who with great presence of mind shut off the steam before he leapt from the engine, by which an explosion was prevented.'

The *Western Times* reported another 'miraculous' escape – that of a mother and her infant. Both were 'flung out'. After regaining her feet it had taken the distraught woman a full ten minutes to locate her child, who was eventually found lying between two of the dead under the carriage. Mother and child were 'very little hurt', declined to go to the hospital and eventually travelled on to Bath, where they were to spend Christmas with friends. [10] Mrs Carpenter, her husband and sister-in-law were also, amazingly, relatively unhurt. Mrs Carpenter said, 'we felt a shock, were tossed against each other, and up into the air and down again, then the carriage broke all to pieces and we found ourselves down on the ground among the luggage.' She said, 'I don't know how my husband got out … then he dragged me out and my sister-in-law. The persons who sat on the right and left of me were both killed.' [11]

Many of the passengers spoke of being 'flung out' (in fact, the accident report says they all were). Being 'flung out' was a potential hazard in any third-class GWR carriage. At that time they were basic, open, wooden trucks with board seating, which was a development from the earliest trucks. The evolution of the railways had been driven by the need to deliver coal, and passengers were very much an afterthought. When the railways arrived, nobody had considered that the common masses would be likely customers. Third-class rolling stock developed directly from the coal wagon, and the earliest versions were devoid of any seating at all (these were generally known as 'Stanhopes'). It was only after some time that a handrail was provided to which the intrepid third-class traveller could cling. [12]

Frederick Smith, Inspector General of Railways, who conducted the Board of Trade investigation, was scathing in his report with regard to the carriages of the train. They were, he said, 'not of such construction as the public have a right to expect.' He pointed out that the seating was 18in high, but the sides and ends of the truck were just 24in, a mere 6in higher – scant protection of any kind. One could have as easily fallen out as been flung out!

Once the news reached London, a train was despatched from Paddington carrying the company engineer, Isambard Kingdom Brunel, along with Mr Saunders, one of the secretaries, and Superintendent Mr S. Clarke, as well as 100 workmen to enable the rescue and deal with the problems. The work to extricate the dead was difficult, hampered no doubt by the amount of heavy, wet earth around. The accident happened at around 6.30 a.m. but the bodies were not recovered until almost two hours later, despite 'every possible assistance being rendered'. Most of the victims were artisans, stonemasons on their way to Cheltenham or Gloucester. They were principally employed by the building firm, Grissel and Peto (Thomas Grissel and his cousin Samuel Moreton Peto) and were working on the Houses of Parliament, Woolwich Dockyard, and other projects. They had all left London as a result of a 'strike'[13] affecting their work. (Strikes had become commonplace during 1841, as the Chartists and political reformers became more angry and radicalised, resorting to taking more robust 'direct action'.)

Eight men lost their lives at the time of the accident. Once extricated they were carried to a nearby workmen's hut to await identification and the coroner. They were placed under the protection of railway policeman, Austin, 'whose task was to wash them and place them in coffins'. Some of the deceased were identified by Grissel and Peto's company foreman, Mr Allen – including Charles Williams (32), and George Mabbot, from Gloucester. Others were identified by their fathers, such as Charles Griffith Sweetland (30), residing at Gloucester, another stonemason but not recognised by Mr Allen; and Richard Ralph (40), whose family home was at Harwill, about 2 miles from Steventon Station on the Great Western Railway, and whose aged father had been expecting him home for Christmas.

John Pooke (30), of Stoke Cannon near Exeter, was formally identified by his father but his name had already been discovered by a letter in his pocket. It was written to him by his 'affectionate grandmother', Mary Pooke, who also resided in Exeter. In it she chides him for not letting his mother know where to write to him, and informs him that 'all here desire to send you their love'. He is described as wearing a drab great coat, a black frock coat, four waistcoats, a pair of dark trousers, two neckerchiefs, a shirt, a pair of shoes and a pair of gloves.[14] Wearing his clothes may have been the easiest way of transporting them, or it may have been his very necessary precaution against travelling slowly whilst exposed to the winter elements. In 1841, it could take anything from nine and a half to twelve hours to travel from Paddington to Bristol. Travelling third class meant that one had little right to anything, as described by *The Railway Monitor*, 'As an individual and a traveller you are one of the lower classes, a poor, beggarly, contemptible person, and your comfort and convenience are not to be attended to.'[15] *Punch* magazine returned often to the plight of the poor third-class passenger:

> The sorrow of the third class man,
> Whose trembling limbs with snow are whitened o'er,
> Who for his fare has paid you all he can:
> Cover him in and let him freeze no more.
> This dripping hat my rootless pen bespeaks;
> So does the puddle reaching to my knees;
> [Some companies bored holes in the floor to combat this problem.]
> Behold my pinched red-nose, my shrivelled cheeks;
> You should not have carriages such as these.

This was no exaggeration. There were stories of people being found frozen to death once the train arrived at its destination.

Joseph Hands (26), was not a stonemason but a painter, residing at Clarence Gardens, Regent Street. He had been on his way home to Cheltenham for the holiday. He was initially identified by a quarterly

The early third-class waggons give a particular interpretation of 'air-conditioned', being totally exposed to the elements. This one is a later development since there is obviously some seating arrangement. Most railway companies believed that this class of passenger had no rights whatsoever.

ticket for December 1841, issued by the Wesleyan Methodist Society, with his name on it. He was travelling with his friend, Jabez Cleeve (several different spellings of this surname), who lived in Cannon Row, Westminster. He, too, had a card for December from the Wesleyan Methodist Society, and was initially thought to be a preacher, perhaps because he was 'respectably dressed'. He was identified as a stonemason by Mr Allen and by Joseph's father, who had to identify the badly mutilated body of his son. There was also a 'labouring man, dressed like a "waggoner" but not yet identified', who was probably William Thomas, another stonemason. He and Charles Sweetland had been working on the Temple Church.

Those who went to the hospital and had to be detained were: Thomas Wheeler (30), a newspaper reporter, from London who had contusions to the face, whilst his wife, Ann, had a broken arm, and contusions to head and back; John Sainsbury, a navigator from Lambeth who had severe contusions all over his body; another with all over body contusions was Anthony Batten (43), a saddler, who lived in Marylebone. Many, if not all, of the passengers suffered from 'contusions' of some kind. (Commonly known as bruises, contusions come in three different grades. The most common are soft tissue bruising, which we all experience at some time; then there are muscle contusions and, more seriously, bone contusions.)

Two of the more severe cases were: Thomas Hughes (15), an apprentice painter residing at Hammersmith. He sustained concussion to the brain, contusions to the face and injury to the abdomen. He was described as 'a bad case'; and Richard Wolley (name found on a letter in his pocket), another stonemason. He suffered a compound fracture of the skull. He was operated on immediately, the surgeons performing a procedure known as 'trepanning' (opening the skull), but remained unconscious. Days later it was reported that he had contracted erysipelas (an infection of the skin that appears as a red, hot, swollen rash), but that this had been successfully combated and he was, surprisingly, still improving. However, a report in *The Examiner*, on 1 January 1842, reported that he had always been 'despaired of' and had died on the Tuesday. This brought the final count of the dead to nine.

Thomas Hawkins from Fishponds, Bristol, again a stonemason employed at Woolwich Dockyard, sustained a dislocation of his big toe, part of which had to be amputated. James Stapleton (31), and William Baldwin (53), also stonemasons returning to Cheltenham, sustained a dislocation of the shoulder and a fracture of the ribs respectively.

The three injured women, identified as travelling alone, were all servants: Elizabeth Barnes (20), residing in the City, had a laceration of the scalp and a contusion of the back; Elizabeth Carpenter (29), from Blackfriars Road, had contusions to her legs; whilst Hannah Cooper (40,) of Kennington Common, suffered dislocation of the bones of the right foot. It may have been Elizabeth Carpenter or Hannah Cooper who was found in 'a kneeling position ... entreating to be extricated'. It was found that she was pinioned, possibly by the main beam of the truck on her legs but, because of the balance of the soil, it was a dangerous process to extricate her and it took an hour and a half before the poor woman was released.

The inquest was opened that same afternoon in a small inn named 'Shepherd's House'. This was a common practice at the time, and the jury comprised twelve people from Sonning. The coroner was Mr James May.

Mr Edward May, surgeon, reported that he had been sent for and arrived at the cutting at approximately 8 a.m. He saw, at that time, eight dead bodies. He believed they had all died instantaneously. All the bodies had sustained injuries. The first had both arms and legs broken; in the second case, both legs were fractured; the third had similar injuries; the forth displayed a fractured skull; the fifth, fractured ribs; the sixth, fractured ribs and collarbone; the seventh, compound fractures of both thighs, together with fractured ribs and pelvis; the eighth had a fractured chest and other injuries. He finished by adding that, of course, he 'need not say that those injuries exhibited were the cause of death'.

Thomas Reynolds, the engineer, (now known as 'the engine driver' or 'driver') took them through his journey. He stated that he met with no obstruction until he came near to a wooden bridge which crosses the railway; here an obstruction was caused by the slipping of the embankment through which the railway was cut.

The consequence was that the engine was 'turned off' the line and 'the carriages turned over'. At the time that this happened, the train was going at its 'usual speed', namely 16–18 miles an hour (this was a good rate for a goods train, but not, perhaps the 'undue velocity' that, it was suggested, he might have undertaken since he was running approximately ten minutes late). When the accident occurred it was very dark and he could see hardly anything. He confirmed he had been shown the 'all was right' lamp by the policeman about half a mile before the slip. He had noticed previous slips in the vicinity but did not think them of any consequence.

When George Hansam, the guard, gave his evidence he confirmed that the morning was very dark, and declared the 'engine man was perfectly sober' and 'there could be no grounds for attaching blame to him'. (The engine man was always the one first looked at for blame.) He stated that he believed the earth fell as they were passing because he was nearly 'smothered from the quantity of earth that fell', but, as it was so dark, and he could not see, he could not be sure. He also said the engine and tender had passed beyond the slip before stopping.

Mr Thomas Bertram was Brunel's assistant engineer, and it was his responsibility to check this section of the line between Reading and Paddington. He told the Court that he did this on a daily basis, travelling down and back. There had been a slip a short time since, but he had taken the necessary steps to prevent any 'evil consequence'. He went on to say that there were employed foremen along the line, whose duty it was 'to report direct to him constantly the state of the works' and, if it was urgent, to take the necessary action themselves. So he was quite sure that the slip was a new one. Brunel was also of this opinion. He told the court that he had seen the previous slip and that the 'usual methods had been applied'. That is, leaving the slip open to drain, so he did not 'apprehend any danger from it'. After the accident, he had pointed out to Mr Bertram the drain which had been cut round the previous slip, and which 'was quite apart from the new one'.

Thomas Bottrill was one of those employed to report on the line, and he stated that he had seen the cutting where the slip had taken place at 5 p.m. the previous evening, and it was fine. George Higg, who worked under Bottrill, confirmed that he had walked that section every day, and had done so at least five times that day, and seen nothing that looked like a problem. He usually walked that particular spot at around 6 a.m. each morning, but on that particular day, the train had not arrived at that time (it was ten minutes behind time). Whilst none could say when the landslide actually occurred, it was suggested that it must have been between the period of 4 a.m. and 6.30 a.m., as the 'up-night' mail left Bristol at 1 a.m. and passed though the cutting at 4 a.m. without any mishap. The foreman of the jury, Mr Miller, requested that the inquest be adjourned, as it had been intimated that there had indeed been a slippage at this very place, some two or three weeks earlier, which would have a bearing on the case, and that the matter should be investigated thoroughly since it was 'most desirable the public mind to be set right on this point'.

The Inquest resumed on the Monday, when passenger John Williams, a stonemason who lived at Cheltenham, gave his tragic testimony. He told that he had been travelling with his son, Charles (24), also a stonemason. His son was in the first carriage and he in the second when suddenly there was a 'dreadful shock' and he found himself on the ground. Coming to his senses, he looked for his son. What the poor man saw would test the strongest. He found his son 'hanging by the neck under one of the wheels, the wheel on his throat. He was quite dead as was another laying near him.'

Thomas Carpenter, of Gray Street, Blackfriars, and John N(?), of Hanham near Bristol, told how the train had proceeded in 'a regular manner'. However, when the engine was stopped by the falling earth, 'the carriages in the rear were forced over those that preceded them and the shock was so great they were thrown out.' There then followed much discussion about the position of the passenger carriages, and whether the passengers had been placed in danger by being put immediately behind the engine. Interestingly, a witness had told how the passenger trucks of the luggage train travelling on the day following the accident, had their positions as eighth and ninth from the engine. *The Times* reported, 'In the present instance it appears clear that if the passenger trucks had been the last in the train, no lives would have been lost, because not one of the luggage carriages were off the line.'

There had been a lot of debate in the papers, and questions in Parliament about the position of passenger carriages (always third class) on luggage and mail trains, as these were particularly heavy trains and, indeed, whether passenger trucks should be part of 'goods' trains at all. The GWR was one of only two railway companies that did this.

In September, just a few months before this accident, a passenger travelling on the GWR's 'up-mail' early morning train (which was involved in another accident because of a slippage at an embankment before Wootton Bassett) had written to *The Times*, stating that he believed the only reason he was alive was because he was in a carriage further back. (The line-up was the *Rising Star* coupled to the *Tiger*, then two second-class carriages, followed by a first-class carriage.) He believed the double-headed engines took the brunt of the force of hitting the earth. The carriages before him had telescoped, one into the other, and the first carriage, between the engine in front and the carriage behind, was where the injured passengers were. He also wrote:

> I observed on my way up a luggage train in which the passengers are placed next the engine – now if any accident should happen to the engine, all who should have the misfortune to be there would for a certainty be killed by the tremendous weight which is following them. Why are passengers put before and not behind the luggage trucks?[16]

Brunel gave detailed information about the reasoning behind the positioning on the fateful day. It was, he said, standard practice to put passenger trucks next to the engine, 'because of the danger to which a luggage train is considered most liable – that is being overtaken by another train in consequence of it being slower.' (i.e. being hit in the rear-end by the following train – 'rear-end' shunts were notorious in the railway world.) Mr Saunders supported Brunel, remarking that 'the general opinion of scientific and practical men, and even of the

Inspector-General, was the best place for passengers in luggage trains was next to the engine'. A very heated letter appeared in *The Times* in response to this testimony, stating that it would appear that 'low-class passengers are placed in unnecessarily dangerous positions [whilst] ... luggage is more protected'. It was a view shared by many.

Among the witnesses were several local persons, who came forward and gave some controversial and uncomfortable evidence against the GWR. Robert Hanning, a labourer resident of Sonning, informed the court that, a fortnight previously, he had seen a 'slip of earth and some draining tiles at the top, at the very spot where the earth fell'. He stated that he had passed twice a day, since the fortnight, and seen no one working in the cutting. He went past early in the morning and late at night when it was dark. He did not know if there had been any repairs or whether the soil he had seen was the soil that had been cast down.

Thomas Goodchild also told the court that there were slips at precisely the same spot where the accident happened, or thereabouts – one on the right and one on the left. He saw two men that same day at work, but when he went six days later, whilst the soil was put back from the rail, 'the break in the soil was not made good, it had remained in the same state since.' Mr Edwin Gosling of Sonning, Mr Thomas Stokes of Swinton, a barrister, and John Plant, a gamekeeper of Sonning, all gave evidence that they had seen, from the wooden bridge, various 'slips' and 'bulges' in this area.

Mr Walter Bridges, who worked as a labourer on the line, confirmed that there had, indeed, been a slip some two or three weeks previous, and that he and four other workmen had been employed to lay a drain, repair it and make it secure, which they believed they had done. He said the company had placed men at the spot to watch if there was a slip, but they had not watched on that night 'because they considered the slip was safe'.

Such was the evidence that the jury had to consider, and when they returned to the courtroom they had all agreed on their verdict, 'accidental death in all the cases and a deodand of £1000'. The reasons for this deodand, which the coroner was initially reluctant to give, were:

1   The jury are of the opinion that great blame attached to the company in placing the passenger trucks so near the engine.

2   That great neglect had occurred in not employing a sufficient
watch when it was most necessarily required.

Under the circumstances it was impossible for a reasonable man to
doubt that the spot was known to be unsafe … and the very least they
should have done was to keep a watchman constantly stationed in the
immediate neighbourhood.[17]

The practice of 'deodand' was one of those oddities of Old English
Law, whereby any 'chattel' (i.e. object or instrument) that caused the
accidental death of a man (or woman) was *Deo Dand* (given to God),
thereby forfeited to the Crown, who would sell it and use the monies
for 'pious' use. In the early days, it would be used to pay for prayers
or masses for the soul of the departed. The interpretation of this law
was confusing and inconsistent, it (sometimes) being held that the
chattel had to be in motion and even 'going forward' towards the
victim. According to Adrian Gray, in his review of 'Transport and
the Law of Deodand' this medieval practice enjoyed a significant
revival in the early nineteenth century.

In this new technological age, when one would as likely be hit by
an engine, mangled by a machine, or blown to pieces by an exploding boiler, as run down by a horse (very common in the crowded
towns and cities at this time), this became more of a 'technical' for-
feit. The coroner's juries would decide a value for the deodand, and
it became an instrument of compensation (or a 'fine' against the
company/owner) but, as *The Times* argued in December 1840, it was
more likely to be 'awarded for middle class lives lost in railway accidents but not for the working class mangled in factory machinery'.[18]

Deodands became popular with coroner's juries – the *Mechanics
Magazine* wrote, 'Deodand after deodand has been imposed by
honest and indignant juries – deodands surpassing in amount any
previously known to our criminal history …' – however, they were
unpopular with the railway companies, as fatal accidents were not
uncommon. The companies began to challenge this in the courts,

often winning on technicalities. The GWR appealed against their fine and won, arguing that the cause of death was unclear, and that one case had been heard by the wrong coroner.[19]

Sir Frederick Smith's report to the Board of Trade, just one day after the accident on 25 December, must have helped, for he concluded that, 'this accident could only have been prevented by the line being more closely watched, ... [but] there did not seem to have been any urgent necessity'. He stated that there was 'no error in construction ... the vertical height of the cutting at the slip being 58 feet, and the slope being two to one, the base being 115 feet', a 'two to one' was, he thought, acceptable to any engineer.

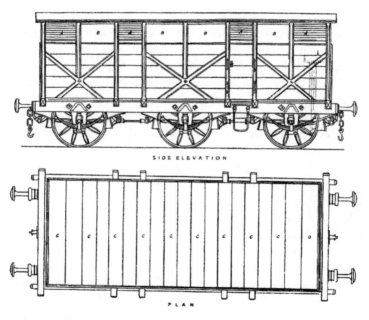

SIDE ELEVATION

PLAN

The drawings for the Great Western Railway's improved third-class carriage, 1844, with references: *A) Fixed Ventilators or Venetians, B) Spaces to be opened or closed by sliding shutters, C) Seats for six passengers each, D) Seats for five passengers each*. As MacDermott drily commented, they have the appearance of a 'milk-van' and as company officials considered that 'the third-class passenger was not likely to be interested in scenery they encased him in a box without windows ... anyhow [he] could not fall out and that was the main thing'.

He believed that, without the excessive rain, the slope would not have given way since it had already held for two years. However, he also said that the accident 'might have been rendered less dreadful in consequences' if the passenger carriages and wagons had had 'spring-buffers', for which he had made strenuous recommendations at previous inquiries. Smith was not alone in his support for the use of buffers, they were a subject of discussion in the mechanical world. Sir George Cayley, scientist, inventor and considered founder of aerodynamics, had written an essay on 'air-buffers' in which he purported that if 'two heavy trains were to meet each other on the same line at full speed – if the elasticity of the buffers be supposed perfect each train would rebound with the same velocity it advanced.'[20] Smith also recommended that the GWR should improve the construction of their third-class accommodation, and make the sides and ends a minimum of 4ft 6in above the floor, and that they should further think about the passengers comfort regarding being exposed to the weather.

The GWR were able to respond quickly to the criticism. In their letter to the Board of Trade of 28 December they inform that these measures 'had already been adopted some weeks ago'. The GWR had, it seems, already ordered several new third-class carriages with the desired heights, which would be 'extremely solid and on six wheels', and have 'greater comfort and protection for the passenger'. Not only this, but they would have the expensive spring-buffers too.[21] In the meantime, until they arrived, they boarded up the sides of existing carriages to the required height.

One thing did not change, however. Despite the Board of Trade writing to the company stating, 'The practice of sending third-class passengers by heavy luggage trains is attended with considerable additional risk whether such passengers are placed next the engine or at the end of the train' and despite their requesting the directors to 'consider a manner that does not expose them to additional danger', the GWR continued to carry them in just such a manner. This was not to change until the implementation of William Gladstone's (then President of the Board of Trade) Railway Regulation Act, 9 August 1844, with all its attendant improvements and protection for the 'poorer classes', which came into force some three years later. Gladstone's 1*d* per mile worker's trains (sometimes known as 'Parliamentary trains') provided seats and protection from the weather, ran at least once a day in each direction, stopping at all stations, and changed the face of third-class travel.

The ineffectiveness of the deodand against the railway companies also influenced further legislation, introduced by the Right Hon. Lord Campbell in 1845, who sought to provide real compensation for victims, and this became the Fatal Accidents Act 1846. (In that same year legislation was also passed whereby deodands were abolished.) A bad accident had effected something good.

3

'BRING OUT YOUR DEAD!'

'**B**ring out your dead!' was a cry that often rang through the streets of historical London, during the frequent visitations of pestilence and plague. At such times of crisis, all niceties would be dispensed with, and the dead brought out and unceremoniously carted away for burial in massive pits slaked with lime to hasten decomposition and to curtail infections. In 'civilised' times the normal practice was for a Christian burial within a coffin, in consecrated ground around the Church which was protected within the wall. For those outside of Christian ideals (such as babes born out of wedlock, unmarried single women who died in childbirth, criminals, paupers and the insane), burial would be on the 'other side', the unblessed side of the Church wall.

In early nineteenth-century industrial Britain, the massive movement from the land to the towns and cities created population explosions and rapid expansions. For London, this was further exacerbated by the large influx of political and economic refugees, e.g. the French running from 'the Terror'; the Jews of various countries (particularly Russia) running from religious and economic persecution; and the Irish from poverty and famine.

Huge social problems erupted, not least of which was how to deal with the ever rising numbers of dead. The small churchyards built for smaller scale communities were being overwhelmed as London spread even further, enveloping the suburbs into the metropolis. There was an outcry, on many levels, from socially-minded Victorians, as more and more official, and unofficial, reports and articles in the papers highlighted the dreadful state of affairs in city and town-centred churchyards.

In 1831, cholera came to Britain. It was the far edge of a pandemic that had started in the province of Bengal in north-east India back in 1826, and had insidiously sent its death-carrying tentacles across the continents. It entered Britain via the ports. It killed many thousands, and overstuffed London and Glasgow, both port cities, were especially hard hit. The talk about overcrowded graveyards became louder and more urgent, but still nothing was done, as an article in *Bell's Life in London and Sporting Chronicle*, in September 1838, shows:

CHURCH-YARDS IN LONDON – HORRIBLE DEATHS – The state of the churchyards of the metropolis is at once disgusting and dangerous, and calls loudly for Legislative interference. To know that the population of London is exposed to the pestilent miasma of our burial grounds, situated as they are in the very midst of the most densely crowded neighbourhoods, is calculated to excite the most painful apprehensions for the public safety. A grave was opened in Aldgate churchyard on Friday, and immediately the pestilential exhalations destroyed the grave-digger, and also another man who went, after a considerable time, to his aid. Let any one read the following evidence before the Coroner's inquest, and say whether it is not the duty of all interested in preserving the metropolis from disease in its worst forms to interfere to stay the plague … Whether partiality for the place, arising from religious or family attachments, or regard for vested interests in those who have a property in the soil, tend to perpetuate the evil, it is obvious that the public health is the supreme law, and the legislature must interfere to preserve it.

Nearly a decade later, and the burial practices had not changed because the necessary 'interference' had not occurred. Many now sought to bring that about. The sole purpose of 'The National Society for the Abolition of Burials in Towns', formed in 1845, was to petition

Parliament for the immediate closure of burial places within cities and towns. They strenuously advocated the discontinuance of 'burying the dead in the midst of the living'. Their cry was 'bring out your dead – way out of the towns and cities and out into the countryside'.

In that same year, Frederick Engels, German social scientist and political theorist, published a social treatise entitled *The Condition of the Working Class in England*. It makes horrific reading, not just regarding the living, but also regarding the dead. Engels writes:

> As in life, so in death. The poor are dumped into the earth like infected cattle. The pauper burial-ground of St Brides, London, is a bare morass, in use as a cemetery since the time of Charles II, and filled with heaps of bones; every Wednesday the paupers are thrown into a ditch fourteen feet deep; a curate rattles through the Litany at the top of his speed; the ditch is loosely covered in, to be re-opened the next Wednesday, and filled with corpses as long as one more can be forced in. The putrefaction thus engendered contaminates the whole neighbourhood.

Such malpractices were not limited to St Brides. Richard Kelsey, Surveyor to the Commissioner of Sewers for the City of London, stated in a Parliamentary Report of 1845 that it was even known that where sewers ran under the church building, these were broken open and bodies placed there. The clergy responsible for the accommodation of the dead were often desperate or unscrupulous (burying was, for them, a pecuniary enterprise after all) and it was not unknown for them to place bodies under the floorboards of the chapel. This would soon be realised by those kneeling and praying above, when the foulness of the smell invaded the room. Dr John Simon wrote several City Medical Reports. In his report of 1849, he highlighted this gruesome and unhealthy practice:

> It is a very serious matter for consideration, that close beneath the feet of those who attend the services of their church, there often lies an almost solid pile of decomposing human remains, co-extensive with the area of the building, heaped as high as the vaulting will permit, and generally but very partially confined ... There are, indeed, few

of the older burial-grounds in the City where the soil does not rise
many feet above the original level, testifying to the large amount of
animal matter which lies beneath the surface.

It was an appalling situation and London was definitely in crisis.
Something needed to be done.

In 1848 cholera came again and killed in even larger numbers.
Some say that 50,000 died, and London graveyards went into melt-
down. It caused the Board of Trade to investigate, what John Clarke
neatly calls, London's 'acute burial congestion' in his comprehensive
book, *The Brookwood Necropolis Railway,* and in its report (1849) the
Board of Trade proposed that a 'London Cemetery' be created outside London, perhaps bearing in mind Dr Simon's findings:

> The use of some spacious and open cemetery at a distance from the
> City should be substituted for the present system of interment, and the
> urgency of this requirement will be demonstrated all the more cogently,
> when it is remembered that the annual amount of mortality in the City
> averages about 3,000, and that under the present arrangements every
> dead body buried within our walls receives its accommodation at the
> expense of the living, and to their great detriment.

The government did not act on this recommendation, but from
1850–57, starting with the Metropolitan Interments Act, a series of
Burial Acts enabled the closure of town churchyards to further burials, and created the mechanisms for the establishment of municipal
graveyards in 'open spaces' outside London and other towns.

The London Necropolis and National Mausoleum Company,
latterly known and more commonly referred to as the London
Necropolis Company, was the brainchild of Sir Richard Broun and
Richard Sprye.[1] These two had floated the idea back in 1849, but
not until 1851 did they register their proposal 'for the formation of
a Necropolis and Mausoleum for the general interment of the dead
... at a very ample sanitary distance' from London and its suburbs,
making generous allowances far above any anticipated expansion
and growth in numbers – dead and alive.

The site they had selected for the cemetery was a large tract of low value common ground at Woking, some 23 miles (37km) from London, which could be purchased from the estate of Lord Onslow. Whilst this would appear to be a ridiculously long way away, the brilliance and novelty of the idea lay in its proposal to use the railway to convey both bodies and mourners directly to the site. The existing London & South Western Railway (L&SWR), established in 1838, already ran from London to Woking and could be easily adjusted to run directly to the cemetery. This, Broun and Sprye argued, could be done more quickly, more cheaply and with less inconvenience than by the usual horse-drawn hearse service through the crowded streets of London to the eight cemeteries just outside its boundaries. They won their argument and the company was incorporated, by private Act of Parliament, in June 1852. To prevent the L&SWR from exploiting its monopoly on access to the cemetery, the act bound the L&SWR to carry corpses and mourners to the cemetery in perpetuity; set a maximum tariff which could be levied on funeral traffic and declared such arrangements to last without any reference to the shareholders wishes. It did not specify detail of how the funeral trains were to operate.[2]

The L&SWR were very happy to be part of this new enterprise, believing that they stood to make something in the region of £40,000 a year in extra fares, but decided that, in order not to alarm their everyday passengers, who might feel anxious about travelling in the company of the dead, the necropolis trains would have to be run as an entirely separate service, with its own rolling stock and timetable. Whilst it would not be the first railway to transport both bodies and mourners to their destination, the Necropolis Railway would be the first dedicated funeral line with a dedicated station, as a small article in the *Carlisle Journal*,[3] in October 1841, reports:

Since the opening of the Brighton Railway several funerals per railway have taken place, the bodies being placed in hearses on the line and the mourners accompanying it in the railway carriages.

Broun's vision for his 'City of the Dead' went outside the dictates of contemporary thinking. He saw it as a 'last home and bed of rest' for all – 'the high and low, the mighty and weak, the learned and ignorant, the wicked and the good, the idle and the industrious' and believed they should lie 'in one vast mingled heap … together.'[4] (The description of 'mingled' is an unfortunate choice of word, as often in the nineteenth century, paupers and others would indeed be 'mingled' together in the same pit, or, perchance, even the same coffin, for want of space!) For others, whilst that may be fine once they were in the ground, how they got there was another matter.

The Bishop of London, the Reverend Charles Blomfield, was one of those, and when questioned by the House of Commons Select Committee in 1842, had not only strongly disagreed with the idea of travelling to one's burial place in a train, he violently objected to any possibility of 'persons of opposite character [being] carried in the same conveyance', such as 'a profligate' with a 'respectable member of church', which would, he declared, seriously 'shock the feelings of his friends'. Such delicacy was something that the London Necropolis Company (LNC) had also thought about and they set up, much to the amusement of *Punch,* what they called the 'Railway System of Interment'. In other words, burial by railway class (first class, second class, third class), and this started, like all other railway journeys, at the departure station.

An article in *Leisure Hour* (1856) reassured its readers that all using the 'Railway System' received the same treatment no matter what their background, 'with but the most trifling difference, the various class rooms are furnished precisely alike … there is the same privacy, the same quietude, the same respect for poor as well as rich.' Further details of the arrangements, however, show that they were very definitely different. On the road level are 'the range of third-class waiting rooms, well and appropriately furnished.' (Note the word 'appropriately'). 'A massive and handsome staircase of stone leads to the next floor, which is devoted to the use of second-class funerals; it then ascends to the third floor, level with the railway platform, and on which lie the first class reception and waiting rooms'.[5] Once at the cemetery, however, every 'class' of dead, even paupers, had their own guaranteed burial space.

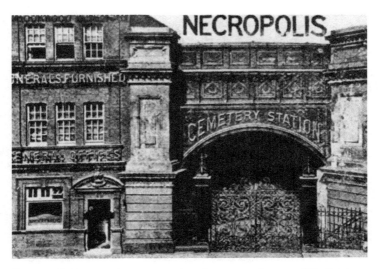

Cemetery Station – was there ever a station of a more macabre nature? Death is in the air as the company offices at 188 Westminster Bridge Road building emblazons the sign 'Necroplis Brookwood Cemetery'. The beautifully designed gates by Messrs Bailey add to the atmosphere. (John Clarke)

The LNC decided that the best location for the London terminus of 'the black line', as *The Spectator* called it, was Waterloo; its close proximity to the river and its water transport system being an added bonus. Work started on the first private necropolis station in May 1854, in an area between Westminster Bridge Road and York Street, and between arches 225–232 under the mainlines of the L&SWR, going into Waterloo. It was completed in October 1854 at a cost of £23,231 14s 4d. It had its own private access road which ran in from Westminster Bridge Road and out on to York Road, which allowed mourners to arrive conveniently and for the discreet disembarkation of the coffins from the hearse and delivery to the train; and, when volume of trade increased, for no holdups from vehicles having to turn around to go out. Both entrances had gated archways – that on the Westminster Bridge side was the more elaborate, also having the distinction of a pair of beautifully crafted iron gates, designed by Messrs Bailey, and originally made for the Great Exhibition in 1851. There were two designated lines enclosed by a shed.

A beautiful Victorian advertisement produced by the London Necropolis Company for the front cover of their brochure of 1899, showing a romanticised view of the funeral train at the cemetery grounds. Note, however, the link with 'modernity' with the telegram code and telephone number up in the top left-hand corner. (John Clarke)

During its lifetime, the York Street Station underwent a number of expansions and changes. Some were cosmetic, such as lining the arched entrance with white lightly glazed tiles, to dispel the gloominess of the approach. Others were more significant, such as the removal of the western wall of the shed, substituting it with an awning, in 1876. An extension of the platform occurred in 1877 and, more significantly, in 1889–90 the encroachment of the L&SWR's enlarged 'A' signal box gantry, which needed to use the Waterloo end of the platform on which to site one of its new iron support stanchions. The major change came in 1899 when, desperately needing the site for its own expansion, the L&SWR agreed to provide the LNC with a completely new terminus at 121 Westminster Bridge Road (afterwards known as the Westminster Bridge Station), with a four-storeyed building, which also housed the LNC's offices. This latter station continued to serve the company until it was hit in one of the heaviest air raids over London, during 'the Blitz' in the Second World War.[6]

The LNC's cemetery, 'Brookwood', was consecrated on
7 November 1854, but did not open to the public for another
week, on 13 November. It had its own branch line and two stations, 'of a character as may be completed within a few weeks'.[7]
The 'North Station', within the Nonconformist section, was nearest the L&SWR's main line, the other, 'South Station', was located
in the Anglican consecrated area; both conveniently situated for the
chapels. As well as the refreshment rooms, which would provide
luncheons for the funeral parties, and serve alcoholic drinks, there
were waiting rooms, 'pauper' rooms, toilets and living accommodation for staff of the cemetery. (Later these stations were used merely
as refreshment 'Bars' but remained in use until the 1960s/70s.)

The Necropolis train supposedly ran every day (including Sundays,
until the 1900s), but in reality it ran 'as required' – no funeral, no
train – departing from London at 11.20 a.m. (11.50 a.m. from the
1870s) and departed from the cemetery for the return journey at
2.30 p.m. There were definite 'regular' trains on a Tuesday and Friday
which could be used by the general public, but these were principally run to accommodate agreements with London parishes to take
the unclaimed dead from their institutions and for 'pauper burials'.

Initially, the LNC used funeral directors but very soon began to
offer their own 'full service'. A rather wordy, but very informative,
advertisement appeared in *The Times*, 6 June 1856:

NECROPOLIS – Established by Parliament – WOKING
CEMETERY –The Company act also as Undertakers – FUNERALS
PROVIDED complete, including private grave. Statuary work, and
every expense, as follows:– First Class £21 0s. 0d. Second Class £18
0s. 0d. Third Class £14 0s. 0d. Fourth Class £11 0s. 0d. Fifth Class £4
0s. 0d. Sixth Class £3 5s. 0d.

The above charges include the performance of the funeral from
the house, with the usual furniture and attendants, but they may be
considerably reduced by dispensing with the funeral cortege through
the streets of London, and the Necropolis Company think it right to
state that the arrangements of meeting at their private station in the
Westminster Road has been introduced by them to relieve the public

from unnecessary and costly display, and that it is now daily adopted and gives complete satisfaction.

Apply personally or by letter to the Secretary, 2, Lancaster Place, Strand, or any agent of the Company, either of whom will wait on the parties and undertake all the arrangements. The train leaves the Westminster Station daily at 11.20. Separate waiting rooms.

The company would arrange all – even sending out the invitations to attend! By 1870, the advertisements had become more concise, more simplified. One, in *The Standard*, 28 November, declared:

Funerals by Railway
The NECROPOLIS is accessible from London in 50 minutes by special train from the Westminster Road Station or by South Western train to Brookwood.

All expensive pageantry may be dispensed with and funerals conducted with simplicity and economy unattainable elsewhere.

Whilst the 'class' of the travel ticket also decided the class of funeral, the site of one's final resting place was determined by one's beliefs – a member of the established Church of England, Conformist or Nonconformist. Being associated with any particular parishes, guilds, societies and communities would also decide one's position within the cemetery. It was divided into many sub-sections, or 'Allotments' as the LNC described them in a brochure of 1890. There was, for example, 'Actors' Acre', inaugurated on 9 June 1858, where both famous and impoverished theatrical persons were buried. The brochure boasts that a 'number of persons who have secured themselves world-wide fame' rest there but the first burial, on 13 November, was that of 'pauper' twin male babies born to Mr and Mrs Hore, of 74 Ewer Street, Barrow, paid for by the Diocese of Winchester.

Those of 'world-wide fame' connected to this book include: Frederick Engels, whose cremation took place at the Brookwood Crematorium; and Dugald Drummond, initially of the North British Railway, but latterly the Chief Mechanical Engineer of the L&SWR. Fittingly, his funeral train was hauled by a 'D15' class 4-4-0, No 463

A travel warrant issued by the Borough of Southwark for two persons to take the Necropolis train travelling third class; presumably family of William Clark. Many such warrants would have been issued to the paupers of the parish. (Southwark Local Studies Library)

— the first of the last locomotive class that Drummond had designed. Engine drivers carried his coffin from his home, in South Bank, to the train which had made a special stop at Surbiton. Alongside family and friends, over 200 L&SWR employees, and many officials and dignitaries of the company, attended the funeral. A memorial Celtic cross was erected on his grave in plot 38, off Church Avenue, and this has been restored in recent times (1994), thanks to the efforts of John Clarke and the local Co-operative Funeral Service.

The L&SWR had distinct areas set aside for its employees of all ranks – first class are located in plot 47, whilst second class reside in plot 48.[8] The Nonconformists were buried in plots adjacent to nos 125 and 134. Clarke lists a number of individual employees along with their stories.

The 'black line' continued to work until well into the twentieth century, although it never carried the numbers so eagerly anticipated by its parent company. Its place in railway history is assured by the macabre character of its existence.

4

'UNBURYING' THE DEAD

With the coming of the railways came also displacement, destruction and even desecration. Not least, when they came to town, and especially when that town was the capital, London. In order to make room for the new, it was necessary to get rid of the old, no matter what it was – homes, hospitals, antiquities and even graveyards. 'Sordid vandalism', as *Punch* termed it; or 'mutilation' as described by historian Jack Simmons,[1] was given political assent – the needs of the railways were paramount. (It must, however, for the sake of a balanced view, be added that the 'clearances' often served the political will of the time and, for many, what came after was sometimes decidedly better than what was there before.)

The feisty Midland Railway savoured a good fight. Born from the needs of 'plain, practical men', who were small coal owners (according to Frederick Williams in his early canonical history of the Midlands), in order to transport their coal, it came out fighting for its territory and its lines, taking on the canal owners even before it took on other railway companies.[2] Some hold, and have written, that it was formed in 1832 with the Midland Counties Railway; whilst more modern thinking finds that what has become known as 'the Midland Railway' came about through the amalgamation of three lines that had a common connection at Derby – the North Midland, Midland Counties, and Birmingham & Derby Junction, in 1844.

Once established, it became a railway of big ideas and big projects. It extended and extended (some, including its own directors often argued that it was 'overextended') in all directions, yet by 1850, whilst it had gained mileage security, it was still a relatively middleweight company. It had a myriad of lines, mostly centred on the East Midlands, with its headquarters in Derby, and whilst its trains ran over the London & North Western Railway lines, via Hampton Junction and Rugby into Euston, it needed its own independent access to London. It did not want to be dependent upon another 'host' and bitter rival, the Great Northern Railway Company, who were imposing heavy tariffs on goods carried by the Midland on its lines into London at King's Cross Station.

A decade later, and with further extensions, the now heavyweight Midland began its push for the metropolis. Eventually yet another extension, from Bedford to London, gave them the independent access they wanted. In 1862/3, the Midland Railway Company secured an Act of Parliament – 'St. Giles's-in-the-Fields Glebe Act' – to build a new London terminus. This was to become known as St Pancras Station – ironically right next door to arch rival, the Great Northern Railway's, King's Cross Station (opened in 1852).

The Midland were always a company prepared to 'think outside the box', for instance, doing away with second-class carriages, when all other companies clung to theirs thinking such a plan was lunacy. They also, somewhat surprisingly for a railway company, thought about the comfort of their passengers. Even in their early life, back in 1842, much to the chagrin of their shareholders who complained it was money ill-spent, they were 'furnishing refreshment and waiting rooms, "more like drawing-rooms in palaces", than places of comfortable accommodation.'[3] Little wonder, then, that when they eventually arrived in London and claimed their place, they did it in the grandest style.

St Pancras, one of the iconic buildings in London, even today,[4] was designed by the company's one-time Engineer in Chief, who was at that time a retained consultant engineer, William Henry Barlow. Barlow's name is most often linked with railways,[5] but he had also assisted Paxton with his design for the 'Crystal Palace' building

for the 'Great Exhibition of Works of Industry and All Nations' in
1851. The Exhibition was a celebration of Great Britain's role in the
advance of modern industrial technology, and the massive 'Glass
House' was a wonderful example of such. It is more than likely that
this experience of grandeur influenced Barlow's thinking when he
took on the design of the Midland's landmark station – that, and the
wish to grandly 'outdo' all other termini in the vicinity. Perhaps not
too difficult against Lewis Cubitt's more functional King's Cross, but
maybe more so against Euston's (the first intercity railway station in
London) ornate tone and spectacular Doric arch entrance, designed
by Philip Hardwick. However, perhaps those that had the most influence were the single span roof designs being built at Charing Cross
and Cannon Street, both designed by John Hawkshaw.

Barlow's (and Rowland Mason Ordish's[6]) finished building was
stupendous. A nation already excited and amazed by ever-increasing
engineering marvels, held its breath in wonder at this new mas-
terpiece. Barlow's design took engineering technology to the next
level, as his immense train shed became the world's largest enclosed
space – a record it held for the next twenty-five years. 'The span of
the roof covered four platforms, eleven lines of rails, and a cab-stand
twenty-five feet wide. It is 100 feet high, 700 feet in length, and its
width about 240 [243] feet … it contains no less than two acres and a
half of glass.'[7] Trachtenberg and Hyman write of it:

> Its 243-foot span was not an exceptional dimension for bridges, as we
> know, but for an interior it was extraordinary, especially extended in
> depth to form the widest and largest undivided space ever enclosed.
> The skeletal transparency of the ferro-vitreous vault added a futuris-
> tic, magic dimension to the stunning space, especially as the vault was
> made to spring from the platform level where the passenger stood.[8]

Whilst the final outcome of the Midland's London station was spec-
tacularly wonderful, (the Grand Hotel there was designed by George
Gilbert Scott) the beginnings were decidedly not. Indeed they were
heavy-handed, cruel and gruesome. The Midland, with the power
to purchase by compulsion or agreement,[9] purchased twenty-seven

The 'first principal' timber staging erected by contractors, the Butterly Company, to enable them to construct the roof of what was to be William Henry Barlow's record-breaking space – St Pancreas station. It was to be a record that would hold for the next twenty years. The day work rate for men working on the job as laid down by the Midland Railway in the contract was – per day of ten hours – labourers 5s 2½d, plumbers 8s 4d, slaters 7s 11d. Whilst the roof was spectacular with more than 2½ acres of glass, the interior was initially quite rudimentary with simple raised platforms either side of numerous lines of rails.

acres from the Ecclesiastical Commissioners, and further acres from the Lord William Agar's estate. The site the Midland had obtained was known as Somers Town and included Agar Town (in the Parish of Old St Pancras), and the graveyards of St Pancras and those of the adjoining church of St Giles. The problem was that the site where the terminus was to be built (according to the wishes of the Midland), could only be approached by tracks that would cross already heavily occupied ground. This was ground which was filled with houses and occupied by great numbers of 'slum dwellers', a canal, a much polluted river, a gas works, a newly built church and a very old and greatly over-inhabited graveyard.

Old St Pancras Church was a venerable antiquity dating back to around AD 600. It is believed to be possibly the earliest site of Christian worship and burial. It had had a chequered, and sometimes beleaguered, history – and it was about to have so again, thanks to the Midland. Writing in 1854, social researcher George Godwin, when addressing 'the graveyard question' (which had by that time been debated for a number of years), wrote:

The appearance presented by the ground of Old St. Pancras' parish is very extraordinary … An account of the number of bodies here deposited would startle the most apathetic. St. Pancras' ground is truly a distressing sight. The stones – an assembly of reproachful spirits – are falling all ways; the outbuildings put up on its confines are rent, and the paved pathways are everywhere disrupted, such is the loose and quaking state of the whole mass. The practice of pit-burial is still continued in this ground. When we were there last, we found a hole with six coffins in it, waiting its complement of about double that number![10]

Not long after this the Act which prohibited any further interments in churchyards within towns and cities came into force.

Less than a decade later the Midland swept into town. 'For its passenger station alone it swept away a church and seven streets of three thousand houses,' wrote Frederick Williams in his *History of the Midland Railway: A Narrative of Modern Enterprise.* (Now it is thought to be more like 4,000 houses.) 'Old St Pancras churchyard was invaded, and Agar Town almost demolished.'[11]

The Midland held that they displaced just 1,180 'labouring persons'. A more realistic number is believed to be around 32,000.[12] There is no doubt that Somers Town was a 'mean neighbourhood', nor that Agar Town was a truly dreadful, unwholesome place, as

'Scorched earth'– in order to make way for the new, first they had to do away with the old. To create St Pancras Station, seven streets of houses and thousands of homes were swept away and Agar Town almost completely demolished. A general view of the clearance with gas works at the side.

railway engineer (driver), railway guard and railway police constable amongst them. W.M.Thomas, writing in *Household Words* in March 1851, confirms this, stating that AgarTown 'is close to the terminus of one of the great trunk railways, where a large number of men, officers of the company and labourers are employed.'

Whilst the living were easily dispensed with, the dead required a different approach. Once the Midland set to work they discovered a great many bodies needed to be moved out of the burial ground. Special procedures were, supposedly, set in motion. Application had to be made to the solicitors and the engineer of the company, and all work was stopped until an Order could be obtained for the proper removal of the remains. Despite these special procedures, terrible things had already happened in graveyards in London.

Where there was a need to 'unbury' the dead, it was the usual practice 'to place a person in authority there, of some position, education, and feeling, in order to prevent unnecessary violence to the feelings of the living by the unnecessary disturbance of the remains of the dead.'[13] In London, when the railways had obtained 'a faculty for making cuttings through city churchyards', it was the Bishop of London who was responsible for overseeing the decent reburying of the dead. In this instance, however, the Bishop passed it to the architect, Mr (later Sir) Arthur Blomfield. We know something of the nature of this, and what had happened at St Pancras through the writings of novelist and poet Thomas Hardy, in the work *The Life of Thomas Hardy*.[14] Hardy, who had originally intended to be an architect, was living in London, and working as an assistant at Blomfield's well-known and respected firm. Hardy writes that Blomfield confided in him about his concerns relating to how a railway company had previously 'got over him somehow' when 'cutting through a graveyard'. Despite being told that all the bodies removed had been reinterred he said, 'there appeared to be nothing deposited.The surface of the ground lying quite level as before.' Blomfield confessed that he had also heard rumours of 'mysterious bags' being full of 'something that rattled', and of visits or 'cartage to bone-mills'. 'I believe these people are all ground up' he told Hardy.

It was not the only time that a railway had cut its way through a cemetery with dire consequences. Years earlier, in 1844, Frederick Engels wrote:

> In Manchester there is a pauper burial ground in the Old Town on the other side of the Irk. This too is a desolate piece of waste ground. About two years ago a railroad was carried through it. If it had been a respectable cemetery, how the bourgeoisie and the clergy would have shrieked over the desecration! But it was a pauper burial-ground, the resting-place of the outcast and superfluous, so no one concerned himself about the matter. It was not even thought worthwhile to convey the partially decayed bodies to the other side of the cemetery; they were heaped up just as it happened, and piles were driven into newly-made graves, so that the water oozed out of the swampy ground, pregnant with putrefying matter, and filled the neighbourhood with the most revolting and injurious gases. The disgusting brutality which accompanied this work I cannot describe in further detail.

That graveyard was called Walker's Croft, and it served the large and much used Manchester Workhouse (built 1792) in nearby New Bridge Street. Engels writes of the workhouse and the graveyard as viewed from a nearby Dulcie bridge:

> The background is furnished by old barrack-like factory buildings. On the lower right bank stands a long row of houses and mills; the second house being a ruin without a roof, piled with débris; the third stands so low that the lowest floor is uninhabitable, and therefore without windows or doors. Here the background embraces the pauper burial-ground, the station of the Liverpool and Leeds railway, [actually the Manchester and Leeds]and, in the rear of this, the Workhouse, the 'Poor-Law Bastille' of Manchester, which, like a citadel, looks threateningly down from behind its high walls and parapets on the hilltop, upon the working-people's quarter below.

The cemetery was originally a close, called Walker's Croft, part of which had been used as a playing field by the Free Grammar School.[15]

Williams describes, '… mountains of refuse from the Metropolitan dust-bins, strewn with decaying vegetables and foul-smelling fragments of what had once been fish, or occupied by knackers' yards and manure-making, bone-boiling, and soap manufacturing works, and smoke-belching potteries and brick-kilns …' Those that lived there were held to be the poorest of the poor and, therefore, by social definition of the time, the lowest of the low. It has to be remembered that, for these desperate people, this place was their home, and yet for an extra sum of £200 (on top of the original £19,500) paid by the Midland to the owner of the land – for the convenience of not having to deal with the individuals themselves – the slums were totally cleared; the people, being weekly tenants and with no rights in law, were cast out without any compensation.

A fascinating research paper by Steven Swensen, 'Mapping Poverty in Agar Town', shows that not all were 'vagrants' or unemployed, as was often inferred. Amongst the 477 occupations identified for those displaced, were many respectable crafts, tradesmen and women, and, ironically, several categories of those in employment on the railways – railway clerk, railway office-man, railway labourer, railway lamplighter, railway porter, railway lamp maker, railway foreman,

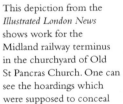

This depiction from the *Illustrated London News* shows work for the Midland railway terminus in the churchyard of Old St Pancras Church. One can see the hoardings which were supposed to conceal the distasteful work of removing the coffins, from passers-by. On the left, men are working on a raised temporary platform of wooden scaffolding which serves as a roadway for the conveyance of the materials to construct the bridge, so that no carts or barrows will make their way among the graves. Frederick Williams (1876) writes of the business, 'On every hand were huge mounds of earth; heaps of burning clay; the fragments of streets; and labourers digging in holes below the level of the earth intent on something; but what that something was, no-one could divine.'

It was sold, by the charity's trustees, to 'the churchwardens of Manchester'.[16] Walker's Croft was consecrated and in use from 1815. It was bought to replace the 'New Burial Ground' which had been used for 'interring poor persons having no family place of burial.' This had become completely full and was closed in 1816.[17] It is often written that many of those buried in Walker's Croft are known to have been victims of the cholera epidemic that hit Manchester in 1832, however, records show that the year in which the high numbers of burials excited a separate entry was, in fact, 1830 – the year a typhus epidemic came again to Manchester.[18]

From 16th of January 1815 (the date of consecration) to 26th of February, 1835	19,950
From 28th February, 1830 to Oct. 31st 1830	8,352
From Nov. 1st 1835 to February 22, 1839	4,944
Total	33,246 [19]

Walker's Croft burial ground was purchased in 1839, by business magnate Samuel Brooks for the Manchester & Leeds Railway – the chief constituent of the Lancashire & Yorkshire Railway (incorporated in 1847). The station was completed five years later. Manchester Victoria Station was designed by George Stephenson and, when it opened in 1844, it consisted of one long single storey building alongside a platform with a single line bay at each end. 'For the next sixty years it underwent a continual process of enlargement.'[20] It is now believed that a considerable part of the cemetery lies under the existing Platform 2.

In London Arthur Blomfield had learnt his lesson. He was determined nothing dreadful would happen again. So, despite the raised voices of locals in opposition to this 'desecration', and questions raised in Parliament regarding the sanctity of the dead, when the Midland Railway decided to cut through the churchyard and that of its neighbour, St Giles, an action that would require 'the removal of many hundreds of coffins and bones in huge quantities', he set up a system of 'superintendence' that could not be 'got over'. He set a clerk-of-works in the churchyard, who was to never leave during

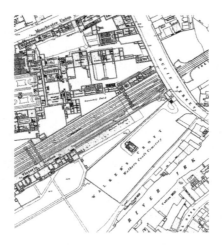

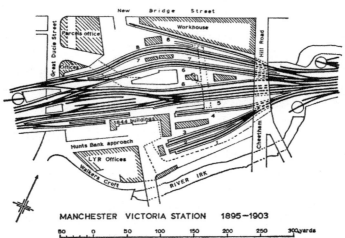

Manchester Victoria Station is built upon 'a pauper burial-ground, the resting-place of the outcast and superfluous', to use Frederick Engels' description. Built originally for the Manchester & Leeds Railway (which was chief constituent of the Lancashire & Yorkshire Railway, incorporated in 1847), one can see the simple 1844 station. The two maps highlight the extensive development over the years.

working hours. As the removals were effected by night and in case the clerk-of-works might be lax or late, he deputised Hardy to go on evenings at uncertain hours, to see that the clerk-of-works was performing his duties. In addition, Blomfield himself was to drop in at unexpected moments during the week.[21]

Hardy attended the graveyard between 5 p.m. and 6 p.m. each evening, as well as at other 'uncertain hours'. There, after nightfall, by the light of flare lamps, and protected by high hoardings that served to hide the grisly proceedings from passers-by, Hardy watched as the exhumations went on and on. Those coffins that held together were carried to the new ground 'on a board merely', whilst new coffins were provided 'for those that came apart in lifting, and for loose skeletons'. It was macabre work indeed. Hardy recalled how, when one coffin fell apart, they found one skeleton but two heads, and that 'the man at St Pancras with two heads' remained a joke between Blomfield and himself even after he had left London and gone home to Dorset to write.

It was well-known that many 'foreigners' were buried in the old graveyards, some of high-ranking status, and another 'black' episode is recorded, telling how they found:

> … the corpse of a high dignitary of the Roman Catholic Church in France. Orders were received for the transshipment of the remains to his native land, and the delicate work of exhuming the corpse was entrusted to some clever gravediggers. On opening the ground they were surprised to find the bones, not of one man, but of several. Three skulls and three sets of bones were yielded up by the soil in which they had lain mouldering. The difficulty was how to identify the bones of a French ecclesiastic amid so many. After much discussion, the shrewdest of the gravediggers suggested that, as he was a foreigner, the darkest-coloured skull must be his. Acting upon this idea, the blackest bones were sorted and put together, until the requisite number of lefts and rights were obtained. These were reverently screwed up in a new coffin, conveyed to France, and buried again with all the 'pomp and circumstance' of the Roman Catholic Church.[22]

This ecclesiastic was not the only notable person buried there. The *Dublin Evening Mail* tells of, 'A host of British and Irish Nobility … many illustrious French, among them princes, archbishops, bishops, and Marshals of France', whilst the *Louth and North Lincolnshire Advertiser* ponders on the seeming indifference to the fact that the grave of William Godwin and his first wife, Mary Woolstonecraft, were to be affected.

That Hardy was touched by this totally extraordinary experience can be seen in his work, *The Levelled Churchyard* – although thought not to be written about St Pancras, the words appear to hit the mark for those poor disturbed souls:

> O passenger, pray list and catch
> Our sighs and piteous groans,
> Half stifled in this jumbled patch
> Of wrenched memorial stones!

This ash tree in St Pancras Churchyard, London, has become known as the 'Thomas Hardy tree' as it bears a plaque explaining his involvement in the dismantling and removal of the headstones, the graves and their inhabitants to make way for the Midland Railway terminus. The jumble of headstones brings home the human reality of the destruction.

We late-lamented, resting here
Are mixed to human jam,
And each to each exclaims in fear,
'I know not which I am!'

Unsurprisingly, perhaps, the Midland Railway was not the only railway company to cause a 'human jam' in their efforts to stake a place in the metropolis. The South Eastern Railway was another. It also wanted to come to town and needed to cross the River Thames into London's heartland at bustling Charing Cross. When they mooted this in 1857, it was viewed as 'a great public improvement ... the benefit to the Metropolis and to the now most crowded thoroughfare ... cannot be too highly estimated,' reported *Lloyds Weekly Newspaper*, in September that year. To enable this to happen, South Eastern Railway formed the Charing Cross Railway Company. The route it would need to take was via Southwark, by St Saviours Church (now Southwark Cathedral), before crossing Hungerford Bridge over the Thames. It meant purchasing a lot of property. On the north side of the river, this included Hungerford Market, a rather cramped site for the terminus and the existing Hungerford Bridge, designed by Isambard Kingdom Brunel and described in glowing terms by the New York Times: 'The bridge is remarkable in having the largest span of any suspension bridge in Great Britain, – 70 feet main span, and two side spans. The cables are chains of bars, and not wire, as in the Niagara bridge.'[23] (Ironically the chains were sold on by the South Eastern Railway to the Clifton Bridge Company for Brunel's Clifton Suspension Bridge.) On the south side the company secured Borough Market, nearby St Saviours Church, as well as sixteen almshouses and burial ground close by. (Cure's College almshouses were founded in 1584 by Thomas Cure, saddler to Queen Elizabeth I.)

The *Morning Post* outlined the route to its readers:[24]

The railway will touch some property owned by the President and Governors of the College [?] of the Poor of St Saviours Southwark. It consists of a number of almhouses built around and enclosing a burial ground. These small houses have been erected with monies left by

Cure's College almshouses were founded in 1584 by Thomas Cure, saddler to Queen Elizabeth I. Almost 8,000 bodies had to be disinterred and removed from the burial ground. They were conveyed by night, on the Necropolis Railway, in specially constructed large boxes which could contain many bodies, to Brookwood Cemetery, Woking.

various charitable individuals ... their windows look out only upon the burial ground as though the donors wished always to keep before the tenants the salutary lesson of their mortality. Leaving these abodes of cheerless poverty ... the railway skirts along the backs of small houses in Park Street and then traverses the Borough-market.

From its beginnings, the new company was very aware of its 'purse-strings' and of keeping to a realistic budget. Right from the first ordinary general meeting, when monies were reported very specifically, it was recorded that, 'railway estimates have proved fallacious in so many cases that the directors have exercised more than usual care in this instance ...' Dr Samuel Smiles (perhaps better known for his railway writings than his position as Secretary of the South Eastern Railway Company) had written reassuringly to the Board of Directors regarding the proposed outlay and possible healthy dividends. Unfortunately, like any railway enterprise, the Charing Cross Railway Company had several nasty financial surprises along the way, especially being forced to purchase outright St Thomas Hospital, its outbuildings and grounds for £296,000. No wonder then, that when they met another totally incalculable 'expense' the person in charge of that operation sought to do it in the most economical way.

The burial ground in front of Cure's almshouses had been there for a very long time, and is believed to have served the parish of St Mary's, Lambeth. All of those buried there had to be disinterred and taken for reburial elsewhere. Edward Habershon was the Architect to the Works in charge of this. His letter to Samuel Smiles regarding the disinterment and removal of the bodies is written in a 'professional' matter-of-fact manner, explaining his actions, calculations and delivery; but such a manner does not overcome the horror of the situation, rather it adds to the inhumanity of it. He writes:

27 October 1862
The College Burial Ground and the Charing Cross Railway Company.

I have now all the accounts of this matter and I send you a summary of them. I have been very careful to keep down the cost or it would have been double from the almost incredible number of bodies buried in the ground. The following short data will give you an idea of the whole:

There were at least 7,950 bodies removed. There were about 5,000 cubic yards of earth removed to the depth of 16 feet amidst an effluvium almost suffocating.

Finding the number so enormous and the cost of separate removal would be so great, I did it wholesale and had 220 very large cases made each containing 26 human bodies, besides children, and these weighed 4 ¾ cwt. There were 1,035 cwt of human remains sent in these cases alone. These were conveyed in the night and the Cemetery Company made arrangements for them. Each body has cost us less than three shillings. It was fortunate that such reasonable terms could be made at Woking Cemetery. [25]

A more horrible business you can scarcely imagine; the men could continue their work by the constant sprinkling of disinfectant powder. Mine was no easy task for the Bishop, the Warden, the parishioners and particularly the relatives have watched the steps taken and the interviews with people and the correspondence has been great but all are more satisfied than could be expected.

I have added my own account ... and I believe I have saved the company much expense ... I shall require a cheque for £200 this week to meet these accounts. [26]

Whilst Habershon wanted £200, the London Necropolis (the Cemetery Company) earned some £1,192 10s – a substantial amount of money from transporting the bodies in the dark of night,[27] albeit at such a modest cost per corpse!

What happened overground also happened under it, and during the construction of the 'Underground' which went across London, the Metropolitan Railway Company also had its encounters with the dead. In 1860, it purchased all of the City Corporation's land on the east side of the 'new' road called Victoria Street, near Farringdon Road. On the west side there had been Ray Street's centuries-old pauper's graveyard. During the development of the road, around 1855/6, the 'inhabitants' of this resting place were in the way, and had been disinterred and transferred to a vault on the east side and thus became the property, and problem, of the railway company. 'The Met' as the Metropolitan was nicknamed, had to battle constantly with the heavily used Fleet sewer, which criss-crossed the route three times, causing problems of logistics, leakage and flooding. In June 1862, a nasty incident is reported:

The creation of the Underground meant that sometimes it had to travel alongside the River Fleet sewer, which caused many problems including leakage, breakage and flooding. In June 1862 the sewer fell in near Ray Street and the flooding was so severe that it caused the collapse of the walls and shorings. It was many weeks before the situation was back under control, and the bodies stored there from previous removals at Ray Street Cemetery would also have needed attention.

Disaster occurred when a section of the sewer fell in near Ray
Street, the tide of sewage inundating the ground on the west side of
Farringdon Road and backing up behind the new retaining wall of
the railway cutting. Despite concerted efforts over the next couple of
days by the railway contractors and the Metropolitan Board of Works
(as the new sewers authority), the wall began to fail, shores and scaffolding across the cutting were smashed and the cutting and tunnel
as far north as Exmouth Street (Exmouth Market) were flooded.
The vault holding the bodies cleared from Ray Street burial ground,
which stood exposed on the east side of the cutting, was broken open
by shoring which had been laid against it.[28]

It took the company several weeks to recover, and what did they do
with the unfortunate dead? Well, we have some indication from a
small article in *Leisure Hour* in respect of a 'trip' taken by the shareholders and members of public institutions affected by the project:

> On the Saturday afternoon named [30 August] the eager shareholders
> and public [representatives of parishes through which the line passed]
> flocked to the Victoria terminus, and after some little delay mounted
> the carriages, first class, second class, and trucks, that had been prepared
> for them. In about 700 yards, all tunnel, passing under the old part
> of Clerkenwell and Bagnigge Wells, the graveyard of the paupers and
> their workhouse, passing huge black boxes full of bones, which were
> being care-fully and decently removed to some suburban cemetery.

'Unburying', and indeed 'overburying', the dead was an occupational
hazard for many of Britain's nineteenth-century railway companies
– the consequences of which are still being felt today. Recent work
for the Cross Channel rail link required the exhumation of 15,000
bodies from the ground beneath St Pancras Station. New work at
Manchester Victoria Station also required numerous bodies to be
disinterred and reburied elsewhere. A plaque, near Platforms 1 and 2,
commemorates these much disturbed, departed spirits.

DYNAMITE

5

THE DYNAMITARDS

Dynamite! The word itself is dynamic. It conjures up feelings of excitement, power, anticipation, fear, terror. It promises action and delivers destruction, even death. It is, then, hugely ironic that the man internationally renowned for promoting peace is also the man who gave us 'dynamite'.

Dynamite started life as nitroglycerine. This interesting compound was created, accidentally, by Italian chemist Ascanio Sobrero, in 1847, when he worked glycerol with a mixture of nitric and sulphuric acid. The combination produced an oily, colourless liquid which was highly volatile, and so unstable that the merest jolt, friction or impact could cause it to explode. Alfred Nobel (1833–1896), a Swedish chemist engineer, met Sobrero in Paris, some three years after this discovery, and was intrigued by its possibilities. Alfred's father, Immanuel, had already worked with explosives, particularly gunpowder, in his construction of bridges. After Alfred returned to Russia, he worked with his father to turn this new explosive, nitroglycerine, into something more practical and commercial. A downward turn in family fortunes forced Alfred and his brother (Emil) to return to Sweden, where Alfred continued his experiments with the still highly dangerous compound, experiencing setbacks and several explosions along the way; Emil, amongst many others, was killed in one such in 1864. The breakthrough came when

Nobel found that, by using *kieselguhr* (a type of soft rock, containing the remains of particular diatoms with cell walls of silica), which absorbed the nitroglycerine, he had a malleable, more predictable material which could be formed into suitable shapes for different commercial uses. Alfred Nobel called this substance 'dynamite' and patented it in 1867. To discharge the dynamite, he invented a 'blasting cap' or detonator which could be ignited by lighting a fuse. Nobel believed that his new dynamite would bring real benefits as it would cut the costs of many forms of construction work that required blasting, but it would also reduce the number of injuries and deaths resulting from the blasting process. For Alfred Nobel, dynamite was intended to be a force for good.[1] Time has shown that it also became a force for evil, even a 'weapon of choice'[2] to those who wished to create havoc, cause destruction, instil terror and threaten life and limb. It was an invention that was to play a significant role on, and below, the streets of London.

The Underground

The 'Underground', or the 'Tube' as it is often referred to today, is, perhaps, one of the best known, and best loved, of all the Victorian inventions. It is as much a marvel today as it was at the time of its conception. 'Punching the envelope', 'pushing the boundaries' and 'thinking outside the box' are all modern day jargon for going beyond everyday thinking, and, with the Underground, the Victorians did just that, creating the world's first under-the-ground railway.

Why would people even think of such a mad-hatter scheme – trains running alongside drains (another brilliant Victorian endeavour)? Well, London streets were chock-a-block. Crowded with street sellers and their wares, buyers, thousands of different horse-drawn vehicles, hand carts and pedestrians, and, in the midst of this melee, people trying to get to and from work. To deliver a standard above-ground railway into the city centre would have been an exceedingly expensive undertaking, in a period when money for railway enterprises was hard to come by. It would also have caused immense upheaval, displacing a great many Londoners from their demolished homes and businesses – the Underground was, therefore, a brilliant conception. The man behind the plan was Charles Pearson, a solicitor by profession. The Metropolitan Railway Company (or 'the Met' as it was commonly called) was formed by Act of Parliament in 1854, to deliver this groundbreaking project, with Sir John Fowler as engineer. Its purpose and function was to deliver travellers, particularly workers, from the mainline stations at the outer edges of London (London Bridge, Paddington, Euston, King's Cross, Bishopsgate and Waterloo) into the city.

Work began in 1860. The *Illustrated London News*, perhaps to allay worries of the travelling public, wrote sympathetically of the enterprise:

> It is intended to run light trains at short intervals and calling at perhaps alternate stations, and all risks of collision will be avoided by telegraphing the arrival and departure of each train from station to station, so that there will always be an interval of at least one station between trains.
>
> The traffic is to be worked by locomotive engines of a novel and ingenious construction. In order to obviate the annoyance in the tunnel arising from smoke and the products of combustion, the locomotive will have no firebox, but will be charged with hot water and steam at a certain pressure to be supplied by fixed boilers at the termini, and will be furnished with a large heater to assist in maintaining the temperature.[3]

Although it is called the 'Underground', in fact it would be better named 'the covered up', as it was mainly delivered (from Paddington to King's Cross) through the 'cut-and-cover' method, whereby deep trenches were dug into the streets along the route. The tracks were laid in the trenches and 'as the cutting proceeded, the supporting shores were replaced with brick retaining walls and piers, backed with concrete and – for most of the way – covered over with elliptical brick arches or cast-iron girder roofs. A backfill of concrete, with a coating of asphalt, and earth on top, completed the work'[4]

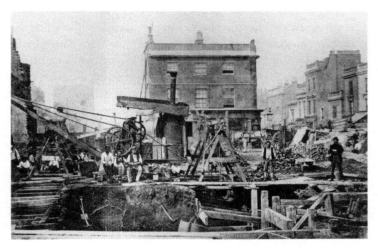

The Metropolitan Railway's Underground was an engineering novelty and marvel. It used a 'cut and cover' method – literally cutting out, then covering over. This depiction shows the workings near Praed Street. It brings home just how 'in the midst of the town' it all was.

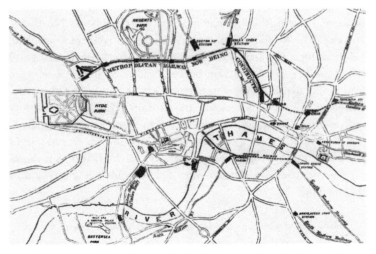

This fascinating map shows the route that the Underground would take, together with the proposed stations – Paddington, Edgware Road, Baker Street, Portland Road, Gower Street, King's Cross and Farringdon Street. It also shows other 'proposed' railway developments, including that of the South Eastern Railway from London Bridge into a new terminus at Charing Cross.

– all strong enough to continue to carry its normal traffic when the road was reintroduced on the top. Some parts, as from King's Cross to Farringdon are in open cuttings (except for a 222m-long tunnel beneath Mount Pleasant, Clerkenwell). It was quick, effective, cost-efficient and a great engineering achievement. (It did, however, create almost as many problems as it solved, caused enormous upheaval and chaos, and put many hundreds of people out of their homes.)

Despite numerous setbacks, with excavations collapsing and serious problems of flooding due to the Fleet sewer bursting, the Metropolitan Railway Company opened its first stretch of underground line for business on 10 January 1863. (The Directors had formally celebrated the completion the day before, travelling along the line with invited guests and then a banquet at Farringdon Street Station.) The slightly less than 4 mile (6km) track ran between Paddington (originally Bishop's Road), Edgware Road, Baker Street, Portland Road, Gower Street, King's Cross and Farringdon Street Stations (it was later extended to Moorgate in 1865).

To accommodate the trains of the Great Western Railway (a major partner in the enterprise along with the Great Northern, and later, the Midland Railway companies), mixed track was laid, i.e. three lines (for standard – 4ft 8½in (1.435m between rails) and broad gauge – 7ft ¼in (2.14m between rails)). So enthusiastic were Londoners for this new, if untried, mode of railway travel that an estimated 25,000–30,000 people travelled on GWR stock pulled by new engines (designed by Daniel Gooch) along broad gauge track that day. Alfred Rosling Bennett, later to become vice-president of the Institute of Locomotive Engineers, recalls the first underground journey he made as a thirteen-year-old boy, only a few weeks after the opening:

> Although laid with the mixed gauge of the standard 4 feet 8½ inches and the Brunel broad-gauge of 7 feet, it was originally worked exclusively on the latter, the G.W.R. providing Locomotives and carriages comprising new features. [They were gas lit.] The engines were arranged to condense the steam they used, or the greater part of it, cold water being carried for the purpose in special tanks … placed

under the boilers, putting the cylinders outside (an almost unparalleled thing on the broad-gauge), to make room for them. For many years the resulting hot water was discharged on the completion of each journey at Farringdon (subsequently also at Moorgate Street and the Mansion House) and replaced by cold. So long as this plan was followed the tunnels were comparatively fresh and clean, but after the Inner Circle was completed and engines ran right round, this frequent change and waste of water was found irksome and expensive and was discontinued, fresh water only sufficient for boiler requirements being taken. This got hot before use, and so ineffective for condensing. The foulness of the tunnels in the later days of steam was quite avoidable, but the Companies found it cheaper to defy public opinion than to trouble about the necessary precautions.[5]

Despite all the drawbacks, the 'foulness', the sulphurous smell, the 'thick darkness', inducing a claustrophobic feeling amongst the crowded hoi polloi (it was an egalitarian experience, where the moneyed mingled with their maids), it was a phenomenal success. It made more of London accessible, more quickly. It made the

The problem of enveloping their passengers with suffocating smoke and steam in the tunnels was a very real one for the Metropolitan Railway. Their engineer, Sir John Fowler, came up with a novel idea for heating the locomotive's boiler with hot bricks picked up at each station. This did not work, so Sir Daniel Gooch refined the idea and came up with something that did – the broad gauge GWR Metropolitan class condensing 2-4-0 tank engine depicted here at the Praed Street junction.

The Metropolitan Underground Railway – proudly presents its stations, interiors and tunnels as shown by the *Illustrated London News* (1862), five months before the line opened.

impossible possible: mass mobility of immense numbers through central London, without congesting its streets, in a much-reduced time and at a modest cost – 6*d* first class, 4*d* second class and 2*d* third class – the 'tuppeny tube' as it was known. This extraordinary achievement transformed London and Londoners' travel habits, (many became 'commuters') and branded London as 'special'.

Its outstanding success ensured its expansion. A House of Lords' select committee recommended an 'inner circuit of railway that should abut, if not actually join, nearly all of the principal railway termini in the metropolis, and the Metropolitan District Railway (commonly known as the District Railway) was established in 1864 to make this happen. This was also a subterranean line using the same 'cut-and cover' method. However, its route was not so aligned to the roads and its costs were much higher (its first section from South Kensington to Westminster cost some £3 million – almost three times that of the whole of the much longer Metropolitan Railway's original line) because it went through areas of higher land values and had more expensive compensation claims. It opened on 24 December 1868, from South Kensington with stations at Sloane Square, Victoria and St James's Park, finishing at what was then called Westminster Bridge.

Initially, all services were run by the Metropolitan Railway until July 1871, when the District introduced its own trains and its 'inner circle' services, starting from Mansion House, travelling to Moorgate Street via South Kensington and Paddington, with trains running every ten minutes. Rivalry and personnel-wrangling between the two companies (who shared three directors and an engineer, Sir John Fowler), held up further development and it wasn't until 1884 that the Circle line was eventually completed.

Whilst all of the Underground is now commonly known as the 'Tube', initially the Tube was something different. It was a deep-level line which was run in tunnels (tubes) dug under London, through its famous clay. It was the preferred option to avoid the costly buying of land and paying of compensation. The City & South London Railway dug two narrow diameter circular tunnels through which they ran the new, cleaner electric locomotives. It opened in 1890.

The Fenians

The nineteenth century was one of transformation. The Industrial Revolution had brought enormous changes in many spheres. New industry opened up new work opportunities, and the railway and the Underground offered new travel possibilities. All offered mobility, up the social scale and around the country and world. Now it was no longer easy for governments to keep the masses in their place – either socially, physically or philosophically – as mobility also enabled a quicker exchange of ideas and attitudes, as well as easier communication.

The world, at this time, was in a state of flux which deepened as the century progressed. 'Troubles', revolution and insurgence provided a hotbed of dangers as the oppressed rose up against their oppressors. Wars, uprisings, assassinations and savage reprisals had smouldered through the decades, but they 'exploded' in many ways in the 1880s and 1890s. During this time Britain, it could be said, was a sanctuary and refuge for those persecuted in their own countries for their beliefs and practice.

'The Victorian public [were] proud of their national tradition of liberal policing and of Britain as a beacon of tolerance, the very idea of political police carried the stigma of foreign despotism', writes

Alex Butterworth in *The World that Never Was*. (It has to be said that this 'liberal policing' or *laissez-faire* attitude did not extend to the indigenous population.) This world of kindly or hostile subversives, of unrealised or potential plots, was a world where 'fiction could so easily be confused with the truth and truth relegated to the realm of fiction' (as in Joseph Conrad's novel *The Secret Agent*, where truth is mixed with fiction); however, according to the Ambassadors of the countries troubled by these *agents provocateur*, it was an unwelcome situation – a 'bolt-hole' or an escape from the 'Arm of the Law'. (It was also a very convenient place to which the same countries could deport all of their 'unwantables', most often without inform-ing Britain beforehand!) London was the centre, not just for Britain, but, claimed the *St James's Gazette*, it was the 'preparing ground for the men who are spreading wounds and panic through the cities of the Continent.'[6]

Nineteenth-century Britain had been experiencing the effects of home grown 'anarchistic' activity for many years (Chartists, political reformers, Mutual Combinationists and Unionists amongst them). All this resulted in a heady and volatile mix, with a maelstrom of ideas swirling around. This spawned radical organisations and groups, often disguised as 'educational societies', all over the country; many of them dedicated to the aims and causes of anarchy. One such was the 'Deptford Educational Society', which held its meetings above a shop in New Cross Road, Lewisham. One of its members was to become notorious.

Despite his intention for good, Nobel's discovery – dynamite – was to play an unimagined role in the provocative agitation by international anarchists (Irish, Irish-American, French, Spanish, Russian and British). Ironically, the 'bomb' became their weapon of choice. August Spies, the editor of an anarchist newspaper in Chicago, put it into words, 'A pound of dynamite is worth a bushel of bullets',[7] whilst the *Dynamite Monthly*, based in New York, whose sole *raison d'etre* was the promotion of uses of dynamite, proclaimed it to be not only 'the hope of the oppressed' but 'their salvation'.

One group who gained an identity (as well as notoriety) through their use of the bomb, in both America and Britain, were the Irish

Republican Brotherhood, more commonly known as the 'Fenians'. In May 1865, the *Leeds Mercury* wrote a long article addressing the topic, 'Who and what are the Fenians?' It said that there were Fenians in Ireland, America and in Canada and asked whether there were any Fenians in Britain. It answered that if there were it was of little consequence. In a very short time, they were to learn otherwise.

The Irish had had a long and troubled history with the English, and had persistently struggled against 'the curse of Monarchical Government', and all the impoverishment and humiliation imposed by foreigners on their land. They had many unsuccessful uprisings and rebellions. In 1858, the Irish Republican (sometimes Revolutionary) Brotherhood (IRB) was created, and in 1859 its American counterpart renamed itself the Fenian Brotherhood. In 1867, they made a declaration of intent 'From the Irish People of the World'. They appealed to all oppressed people (the English workers included), 'Republicans of the entire world, our cause is your cause. Our enemy is your enemy. Let your hearts be with us …' they urged them to take up arms as, 'force is our last resource'. They reassured the English workers, '… we declare in the face of our brethren, that we intend no war against the people of England – our war is … against the aristocratic leeches who drain alike our fields and theirs.' They gave a rallying cry, 'avenge yourselves by giving liberty to your children in the coming struggle for human liberty' and signed off – 'we proclaim the Irish Republic – The Provisional Government'.[8]

Fourteen years later, after acrimonious changes in leadership and fluctuating membership, with many more activists and starving families having fled to America, such 'brothers-in-arms' sentiments were to change drastically. The Irish-American Fenians, with their new sub sects, under new names, (such as 'Clan na Gael' and 'Sons of Freedom') unleashed their war of attrition on British cities and British people and the bomb became what Shane Kenna calls their 'language of political grievance'. Now was the time 'not only to scare, but to hurt England!'[9]

The 1880s have come to be known as the 'Decade of Dynamite', one has only to look at the pages of *The Times* to see that dynamite incidents of one type or another were constantly in the news. So much so, that in April 1883, the Home Office issued a directive to all local authorities and police under the heading, 'The Dynamite Conspiracy', reminding them of their responsibilities and how far their powers went. In his paper, 'The Fenian Dynamite Campaign and the Irish American Impetus for Dynamite Terror, 1881–1885', Kenna discusses the rationale and thinking behind this new wave of activism. It was not, he writes, met by universal acceptance by fellow Irish Fenians and he quotes James Stephens, the founder of the IRB, as finding the suggestion 'the wildest, the lowest and the most wicked conception of the national movement'. Despite this, a 'few bold and devoted heroes' sprang up (as described and urged by Patrick Ford in the radical New York *Irish World* newspaper) to take the fight to Britain.

One such was the Irish born, American bred James Stephens; another, the terror extremist Harry Burton, believed to be head of the 'Avengers Society', whose members, it is said, would kill anyone, friend or foe, upon command – especially 'traitors' to their cause (i.e. spies and informers, particularly those from within their ranks). These men would not fight a battle but would 'keep up without intermission a guerrilla warfare' of skirmishes.[10]

Kenna also examines the influence that the American Civil war (1861–65) later had on the wider culture of warfare with respect to civilian involvement, and the rising role of technology which was, he believes, helped by the easy availability of cheap scientific journals, that instructed and assisted the common man to manufacture his own explosives, rather than have to rely on chemists and scientists. The homemade bomb characterised political attacks in Britain, America and in Europe, and, as such, its nature, performance and outcomes were never fully under control. This was the experience the first time the Fenians used the bomb in England.

Back in 1867, they had blown up part of Clerkenwell House of Detention in London, in an attempt to free an imprisoned leader, but such was their exuberance in the amount of explosive they used that they demolished a large part of the wall and the fronts of nearby houses killing twelve (some immediately, others died of their wounds later), and injuring over a hundred others in the process. It was a criminal (not of terrorist intention) act but still brought fear and alarm to Victorian society. Ironically by this 'non-political' act, the Fenians inadvertently achieved what they never had done before, when William Gladstone publicly remarked how the 'explosion had convinced him to address the Irish question'. This would effectively result in the disestablishment of the minority Anglican Church of Ireland (1869), and the introduction of Gladstone's first Land Act.[11] It was a victory that, unhappily, showed that terror brought political results, and it paved the way for more of the same in later years.

The first known incident involving a bomb, a train and (probably) a Fenian, took place in America on 28 October 1876, when a time-delayed bomb exploded in the luggage carriage of the express train from Philadelphia to Jersey City. It is believed that the bomber(s) had sought to wreck the train and kill its passengers. It was an event that was to have significance in Britain some years later as the bomb (constructed 'with a pistol tied to clockwork which, upon reaching a set time, would discharge the pistol and detonate the bomb')[12] bore a remarkable resemblance to other such devices found at London's Charing Cross, Paddington and Ludgate Street stations. It was this device that would lend credence to the belief that the bombers had been trained at the same 'dynamite school' run by the 'Skirmishers' in Brooklyn, and that these 'infernal machines' were indeed the work of the Fenians. High-ranking Fenian, Jeremiah O'Donovan Rossa, one of the school's founders, claimed its success stating, 'young men have come over from England, Ireland and Scotland for instruction and … several of them have returned sufficiently instructed in the manufacture of the most powerful explosives.'[13] Some of the students were found to be active in Britain during the 1880s. In April 1883, an extensive 'Explosive Manufactory' was discovered, by fortunate and zealous police work, in a small shop in Birmingham, and several Fenians including Albert Whitehead and Henry Dalton were apprehended.[14] In this year, the 'Special Irish Branch' was formed as a temporary measure to deal with the 'Irish problem', but, after three years, the word 'Irish' was dropped and the department continues to this day.

Suspected Attempt to Wreck a Train[15]

On Monday evening, 13 September 1880, an attempt was made by a person or persons unknown to blow up the London & North Western Railway Company's early express 'down-train' from Euston at 5.15 a.m.– or so it was initially thought. The bomb had been placed a few hundred yards from Bushy Station, which is about 16 miles (26km) from the Euston terminus, in the direction of Watford. At this section, there are four lines of rails, the express mainline trains having up and down lines of their own.[16] Happily, the bomb did not explode and the 'near miss' was not discovered until nearly two hours later, when a plate layer gang went out to inspect and maintain the rails. Plate layer John Heath discovered that the fishplates (bars that hold down the rails) had been removed on both sides.[17] Investigating further, he found a brown paper package, partly open and tied with strong cord, placed in a small hole which had been dug alongside the sleeper of the outside rail. Inside the parcel was something that looked like red lead. Heath did not think 'bomb', but rather that the package had something to do with telegraph workmen who had been there, presuming they had gone off to Watford to report the damage to the rails. He did his best to replace and tighten the fishplates without the aid of the necessary spanner, left the package, collected the signal lamps for which he had been sent, and made his way back to Bushey Station. Meeting his 'ganger', Joseph Holwood, on the way, he informed him of what he had found. Holwood immediately went to the spot, secured the fishplates, collected the parcel and the small jemmy lying alongside, and took them on to Watford Station.[18]

The deputy stationmaster's report (the stationmaster was on holiday) to the Superintendent of the Line was clear and precise:

> I have to report to you that platelayer Heath of 20 gang, who was going to fetch the up distance signal lamps, on Monday morning about 7.10 am, found a parcel of some explosive material of a reddish colour, in a hole which had been dug by the side of the sleeper at the joint. The two fish-plates had been taken off and an india-rubber tube filled with gunpowder and long gun-caps fixed at the end, was

attached to the explosive material. A jemmy about 18inches long was also found beside it. Heath says that by the look of the tube when he found it, he thinks that the 'jar' of the train must have jolted the end with the gun-caps in it off the metals [rails] thus avoiding a terrible explosion. It (the explosive substance) was found on the down fast line. The ganger of Heath's gang took the stuff to Watford and handed it to Inspector Keys.[19]

Inspector Keys wrote a corroborative report, which was passed on to the company's own police department at Euston. Railway companies had had their own police working in a law enforcing capacity since 1838, and later also had 'detective' departments. The Great Western Railway was the first, forming their detective branch in 1867. On a case such as this they would have, and did, work hand-in-hand with the local police: Inspector Isgate of the Hertfordshire County Constabulary stationed at Watford; the Metropolitan Police; Detective Warne; and the Home Office Explosives Department. Under the 'The Explosives Act 1875' the Home Office became responsible for enforcing the law with respect to manufacturing, keeping, selling, carrying, and importing gunpowder, nitroglycerine, and other explosive substances. Their representative was, thereafter, part of every explosive investigation, and no coroner's court, relating to explosive matters, could proceed without the presence of a member representing this department.

Superintendent Copping, of the L&NWR, and his detectives went down to make a 'minute examination' and conduct a 'rigid examination of all who could throw any light on the subject', namely, all company personnel. Alfred Boddy, a company employee (probably a lampman from his description of his duty), reported that, on the evening of the day before, he had proceeded at his usual time, around 7 p.m., to attend the lights near the spot, 'and there picked up a portion of lamp such as is used by engine drivers'. The lamp appeared to 'have been recently cleaned and bore no traces of having been on the ground for a considerable time.'[20]

At first, it was thought that it might be the work of 'a discharged or dissatisfied employee of the company', but this notion was quickly

discarded. Then it was suggested it might be 'villains' attempt-
ing to derail and then rob the passengers of the train (an imitation
of American train hold-ups, perhaps) or more probably the work
of 'political conspirators'.[21] The most popular 'conspiracy' theory
was that 'Nihilist' refugees had planned to blow up the train on which
His Imperial Highness, Grand Duke Konstantin Nickolayevich,
would return from Scotland. (The technique used was a close imitation of that used in the blowing up of a train in Russia, in an attempt
on the life of the Emperor of Russia, on 4 December 1879.) Police
inquiries were, for some time, directed to the Nihilist quarters in
London. These enquires were dropped after a letter appeared in *The
Daily Telegraph* sent in by Russian socialists who wrote of their grati-
tude to 'their hosts' (the British), insisting they would not 'jeopardise
the lives of their hosts' (and by implication their own sanctuary), and
pointing out that the Grand Duke 'has so little political influence in
Russia that he is quite safe even in his own country.'[22]

The direction of the enquiries changed after two 'creditable' witnesses came forward, and another theory involving the Fenians came
to the fore. The men, one a watchman at the Sedgewick's brewery
almost alongside the spot, and the other, James Hart, employed at
Messrs Rowe's coal shed near the station, maintained that they had
heard a very loud explosion 'on the Sunday night between 9 and
10 just about the time when the *Irish Mail*, the *Limited Mail*, and an
express train would be passing in rapid succession'.[23]

Apparently the Fenians had threatened action against the *Irish
Mail* previously.[24] The *Irish Mail* was the first train to be named,
back in 1859. It ran between Euston London and Holyhead and
'in 1863 it was the fastest train out of Euston'.[25] These fast mail
trains (and steamers crossing the Irish Sea) initially carried only limited numbers, restricted to first-class and second-class passengers,
and were popular with politicians or landowners needing to get
to Ireland quickly. The *Limited Mail*, sometimes called the *Scotch
Limited Mail* (George P. Neele, superintendent of the line of the
L&NWR called it such) began to accept third class in the autumn
of 1876, but the *Irish Mail* held out.[26] On 1 March 1875, 'sleeping

saloons' were introduced on night runs of the *Irish Mail* for an extra fare of 5s. The guards made generous, if 'illegitimate earnings [from] their custom to furnish likely patrons with sticks and a spare cushion [thereby] ... the space in the compartment was comfortably bridged over, and a long sofa-shaped seat established.'[27]

A search of the company's books for tickets issued did not shed light on any 'illustrious personages travelling by any mainline down-train from Saturday to Monday inclusive,'[28] including any politician. It was, however, later leaked that Lord Northbrook (First Lord of the Admiralty) and his friend a Dr (Sir) Richard Quain had actually travelled on this train, adding to the possibility of a targeted person and train. The *Limited Mail* left Euston at 8.25 p.m. that Sunday night (twenty-five minutes after the *Irish Mail,* ten minutes before the Scotch express and twenty-five minutes before the Liverpool and Manchester express passed through Bushey at 9.15 p.m.).[29]

Having ascertained, through chemical analysis, that the substance was indeed dynamite, the precaution of placing more police along the line, and at Bushey Station, was taken. Altogether, there were found to be twenty-seven cartridges of dynamite, or 'long paper bags shaped like tolerably large sausages resembling miner's charges' as *The Times* described them. Eventually it was determined that the 'sausages' came from Nobel's Explosive Company's works in Ardeer, Ayrshire. The company recognised their products despite the coverings having been torn off and substituted with part of the *Echo*, and inside that *The Telegraph*. It was also determined that they had not been obtained through ordinary channels. The long detonator caps, which were fixed to each end of the three India rubber tubes, were from either Messrs Dyer & Robson, or Ely Brothers Ltd.[30]

One point of interest is in respect of the India rubber tubes. Why? Well, India rubber tubes were accessible to members of the railway staff. An item, in G. Neele's, *Railway Reminiscences*, tells what happened before the company introduced 'first aid' classes:

> Prior to these skilled lessons, it had been arranged to supply 'tourniquets' to all the signal boxes, goods guards' depots, etc.... *Elastic India-rubber tubes*[31] were at first supplied in special boxes, with instructions

as to their being constantly kept supple, and as to the course to be adopted to arrest bleeding in case of accident.

The way in which the bomb had been put together suggested that it was indeed homemade, and by amateurs. Fortunately, it had been a gloomy, wet night on the Sunday and the ground around was very wet, as was the dynamite when found, and so it would not have readily exploded, although the driver of the *Irish Mail* had reported that he 'was conscious of a slight explosion, which he took for a defective fog signal'. If it had exploded, all traces of the bomb would (they hoped) have disappeared and the removal of the fishplates would have led to the conclusion that this was just another unfortunate railway accident amongst the many.

The event raised a lot of indignation in the local community of Bushey and Watford, more outrage than fear, especially the 'un-English' nature of it. Despite the government and the L&NWR each offering a reward of £100, and despite there being promising leads which were handed over to the Criminal Investigation Department, no one was ever apprehended for this crime. One of the leads was, 'a man driving away in a trap around the time'; another was a 'Mr T' who had given a fictitious address at Charing Cross Hotel, when he purchased a similar number of detonators about ten days previously. There had been great excitement about the fact that he had then written to the company saying, 'Mr T thinks that he did not mention the number of detonators ordered by him today … he will want ten'.[32]

There was (is) little evidence to support the idea that this was a Fenian attack. Superintendent Neele also found the idea difficult to accept, he wrote:

The alarm respecting Fenianism still continued, and we had frequent letters warning us that the Irish Mail and the Britannia Tube were threatened. For my part, I had difficulty in believing that any Fenians [would] interfere with the mail in view of the fact that the Irish Members were so frequently travelling by that train.

What is interesting, and also lends weight to the fact that this was not their work, is that none of those who write of the Fenian campaign include this incident in that campaign – it is universally agreed that their campaign started in January 1881. Making the time to disguise it as a probable accident was definitely not their *modus operandi* and, as importantly, would not fit their purpose since, for them, 'the deed' was their propaganda. That the attempt caused such excitement is not surprising, since it was the first ever act of terrorism on the railway in mainland Britain.[33]

The Fenian Campaign

The Fenians carried out their terror campaign from January 1881 to January 1885 (some say 1887), covering one end of Britain to the other. They chose 'hard' targets i.e. those representing the government and the 'Establishment', which included the Houses of Parliament, Scotland Yard and *The Times* offices, this to hurt Britain; and 'soft' targets – the Tower of London, the railway stations and the Underground – to bring mayhem to the masses. There is debate, even today, whether the bombers included civilians in their scenarios – wanting, or not, to achieve their deaths or mutilations. This debate is very much open in respect of their attacks on 'The White Tower', the railway stations and the Underground.

The Fenians started their anti-railway campaign in the North. On 20 January 1883, there were dynamite explosions at Tradeston Gasworks, Possil Canal Bridge and a coal shed of the Caledonian Railway. Then they came to London.

A Daring and Dastardly Outrage

On Tuesday October 1883, 'a daring and dastardly outrage'[34] occurred on the 'Underground Railway'. A 'series' (as they were called by the papers) of explosions took place within a few minutes of each other at around 8 p.m.

At Praed Street Station, it is believed that there were actually two explosions, 'the first so slight only to attract the attention of a few of the passengers.'[35] Mr W. Langridge, a first-class passenger in the affected train, spoke decisively of 'an explosion like that of a fog-signal; a short time before the main one'.[36] The other, a much more dramatic affair, exploded just after the train (made up of the engine and six carriages – two second class, a first class and three third class) had left Praed Street Station, on the up-line, and gone through the first tunnel of approximately 50 yards, into the open for another 30 yards and had just entered the short tunnel before Edgware Road Station. The violence of the explosion was felt on the left-hand side of the train. It blew out all of the lighting on the Praed Street Station platform, in the tunnel, and in the most of the train, which continued in the pitch dark, with its passengers shrieking in alarm and pain and crying for help, until it arrived just minutes later at Edgware Road. Those in the damaged carriages travelled where they had been thrown, 'in heaps together', many were concerned that the carriage would fall apart before they arrived. At Edgware Road, the full extent of the damage could be seen. The last three carriages, all third class, bore the force of the explosion, but the main brunt impacted on the last two carriages, the very last being where the guard's van was located. Mr Langridge later reported that, as the train pulled out, he had looked out of the window on the off-side to check the signals in the six-foot way, as was his usual practice, and noticed 'a stream of sparks like the burning of a fuse under one of the carriages. Immediately afterwards he heard an explosion and was knocked down senseless.'[37] It was in the second to last carriage, however, where the more severely injured were to be found, and the remains of the carriage was covered in blood, with the many blood-stained pocket handkerchiefs left behind presenting 'a most sickening sight'. All three carriages had their left side blown inwards, and the other side blown outwards whilst their windows were blown out in main measure or completely, the glass broken into thousands of pieces, some large, most tiny splinters, and a lot reduced to granular powder, although the floors and main structure remained intact.[38]

Whilst passengers burst out of their first and second-class carriages onto the platform, those in the thirds had to be helped and extricated. There were many injured, bleeding and covered in blood from cuts and piercings caused by the flying glass and wood splinters. The injured were taken to the waiting rooms, but these were already rather full with passengers waiting for trains. Many were travelling after visiting the Fisheries Exhibition (some shrimps were found strewn on the floor of one the carriages, obviously bought at the Fisheries for a later meal). Most of the injured were male labourers and tradesmen, the few women being 'in service' and identified as maids. Dozens were treated at the scene, some twenty-eight were sent on to St Mary's Hospital (the nearest to hand), and many took themselves off once they had 'collected' themselves. Two school boys, Arthur McLintock and Ernest Lindley, up from Clacton-on-Sea for a day's outing, received superficial cuts. Initially the number was reported to be in the region of forty, but the official report finally cited sixty-two, although this was only those who were recorded. Four had injuries severe enough to warrant being detained in the hospital for several days:

Corporal Walter Warren (24) of 4th Queen's Own Royal Hussars, Kensington Barracks, was one of the most badly injured, with very severe wounds to his head and face, and his throat badly lacerated. He remembered seeing 'a very bright flash' followed by 'a terrible report like a cannon. It was on the outside of the carriage. I was struck by something that knocked me almost senseless.' His cap was found in the carriage later and bore traces of its wearer having received a bad blow to the head.

William George (23), ham and beef cutter, of 131 Queen's Road, Bayswater, also suffered bad scalp wounds. He had travelled in the last carriage which was 'rather full'. He remembered hearing two 'reports', a 'very sharp one and the other a dull sound'. He saw 'a flash' and 'the lights of the carriage went out suddenly', then he found himself scrambling around amongst the other passengers. When he 'collected' himself he took out of his head a piece of glass an inch and a half long.[39]

James Turner (16), porter, of 85 Abingdon Road, Kensington, had injuries to his eyes and ankle. He gave his account, 'I was in the last carriage but one in which there was a brake. I saw a very bright light reflected upon the side of the carriage. I was going to put my head out of the window … when I felt my face severely scorched and was thrown back … there was a strong smell … and I was half-suffocated by it. We were in most complete darkness until we reached Edgware Road.'[40]

George Brown (45), coach trimmer, of 9 Talbot Square, Hampstead Road, suffered scalp wounds.

It was later discovered that the tympanic membrane of both William George and James Turner had been partially or wholly destroyed, leaving them either deaf or with severe hearing problems.

Mr A.C. Howard, District Superintendent of police, Mr Godson, of the Metropolitan Railway police, Detective Inspector King, and Detective Sergeant Cloake took evidence from the officers of the company, and examined the tunnel. They found sleepers reduced to matchwood, whilst the rails were not damaged. The roof and walls of the tunnel were only superficially marked, but the gas pipe, about 1¼in diameter, running by the side of the tunnel (to provide low level gas for lighting in the tunnels) had been blown up from underneath, and was twisted. After an initial inspection, the train was sent to Neasden works for fuller examination and the tunnel was sealed off until official government inspectors arrived.

The other explosion occurred on the Metropolitan District Line between Charing Cross and Westminster Bridge stations; some 300 yards from the Charing Cross entrance to the tunnel, and 100 yards below the first ventilator in the Embankment Gardens. Luckily, there were no trains in the tunnel at the time, although there was a train standing at each station. The signalman at Westminster Bridge Station, whose box, over 4 miles from the explosion, was so badly shaken that all its windows shattered, said that, on hearing 'the report', feeling the shock and seeing 'great clouds of dust and smoke pouring out of the tunnel', he looked at his watch which said 8.30 p.m.

The back-blast from the explosion is believed to have been dissipated by the ventilation hole; however, it was still such that it extinguished all the lights in Charing Cross Station and in the train there; it blew over three of the passengers waiting on the platform, and blew out plate glass windows in various parts of the station and its roof.

All train services were immediately stopped, and a thorough search of the tunnel was undertaken by railway personnel. They discovered 'a hole some four feet in length and three feet in width and one foot in depth between the outer rails of the up-line (Mansion House to Kensington)'.[41] The rails, or 'metals' as they were often called in newspaper reports, had remained intact; however, different sets of telegraph wires (vital for informing the next station of the departure of the trains), 8ft and 13ft from the ground, were 'ripped out and hanging, some quite broken. The roof and walls of the tunnel bore marks of having been struck by the flying ballast. Numerous fragments of Plaster of Paris were found around the crime scene, a substance which was known to be used in the making of "dynamite cartridges".[42]

The papers were quick to point out that, whilst these events were a surprise, they were not totally unexpected. It was reported that, three months earlier, the 'Railway Authorities' had been informed by the police that they had received warning from America that the Fenians would extend their 'skirmishes' (as the Fenians termed them), and perpetrate acts of violence on the Underground. The railway companies had already 'taken extra precautions' and were able to start making enquiries immediately.

Those 'making enquiries into the mysterious affair', as the papers reported, were the Railway Police, Scotland Yard, Dr Dupre, advisor to the government on chemical subjects, Sir Fredrick Abel, War Department chemist, and the Home Office Explosives Department led by Colonel Sir Vivian Dering Majendie.

After the bomb exploded in the tunnel between Westminster Bridge and Charing Cross stations, smoke blasted back into Charing Cross Station causing great alarm. Such was the power of the back-blast that it blew out the station's gas lights plunging it into deeper gloom, and knocked over the passengers waiting for the trains.

Majendie, previously of the Royal Artillery, had already written several books on explosive materials and armaments when he became the first to hold the post of Chief Inspector of Explosives, in 1871. He was also influential in framing the Explosives Act 1875. On this occasion, Colonel Majendie was assisted by Captain Cundell. This team carried out experiments, at the Royal Arsenal in Greenwich, which simulated the conditions in the railway tunnel and the supposed substances used. They came to the conclusion that, from the violence of the explosion and the way the force was expended, that dynamite with 'something in the nature of fuse attached to it' was used to commit 'the dastardly act'.

The Report gave its findings:

We beg to express our opinion that:

A That the explosions were malicious and deliberately effected in each case by a charge of the nitro compound (or, as it is more commonly called, dynamite) character

B That the charge did not in either case exceed a few pounds, and, unless an exceptionally weak nitro compound were employed, may in both cases be confidently put down as under five pounds

C That the charge was in each case thrown from an up train – viz – In the Praed Street case from the injured train and in the Charing Cross case from the up train that was just leaving Westminster

D That the charge in the Praed Street case exploded prematurely, the fuse or arrangement on which the retardation of the explosion was to depend having failed to act as intended, a portion of the charge being burnt, and the remainder exploded before the train was clear. [43]

What linked this outrage to other similar recent Fenian incidents, the papers concluded, was the 'savage disregard to life and indifference to the consequences'.[44] That this 'outrage' was the work of 'the Brotherhood' was confirmed by O'Donovan Rossa in America, who also confirmed that they were pushing forward with 'their operations to reduce the English to submission' and advised Britain to watch for 'new developments in their activities at any moment'.[45]

The Home Office and the Metropolitan and District Railways conjointly offered a sizeable reward of 500s. The reward did not help to elicit any useful response, apart from a drunken man claiming, and then retracting, his involvement. The papers later reported that the only outcome of the event was that up to thirty people had lost their hearing to some extent. It was purported, however, that this seemingly 'hopeless situation' was to mislead those whom Scotland Yard were tracking – two particular Fenians – Captain John McCafferty, a well-known Fenian 'head-centre'[46] (term used for commanding officer) and a convicted felon in Ireland now on the run; and William O'Reardon, also a wanted man. It was to be another four months before the railways came under attack again, this time by another 'sec' or 'cell' of Dynamitards.

The 'Infernal Machine'

On Tuesday morning, 26 February 1884, just three minutes after 1 a.m. (according to the number of stopped station clocks found afterwards), an explosion occurred at Victoria Station, the terminus of the London, Brighton & South Coast Railway, and the London, Chatham & Dover Railways. The headline that hit the papers, just a few hours later shouted:

DYNAMITE OUTRAGE AT VICTORIA STATION

The last trains for the night from London-bridge, Clapham Junction and Ludgate-hill had discharged their passengers and the night staff were just starting their usual routine of locking the doors, checking the gas and readying the fire-hose in case of an emergency, as they did every night, when 'a red sort of flash … and a sound like a small cannon' stunned them to the spot. Mr George Manning, the night inspector, witnessing the explosion just twenty to thirty yards away, stated that 'it was as if a small cannon had been fired out of the window of the cloak-room up the platform'. The boom travelled as far as Clapham Junction (roughly 3 miles or 5 kilometres distance) where, extraordinarily, a female attendant from the Refreshments Rooms heard the noise, believed it to be from the station, and came in to help![47] The boom was followed by 'the crashing of the roof, the fall of glass in every direction … and cries of alarm in the neighbourhood'.[48] There was another whoosh of explosion when the gas from the broken gas-pipe ignited and the burning station lit up the dark skies.

The honest Mr Manning did confess that his first thoughts were to take his men and run for their lives, but then decided they needed to 'obey the call of duty' and set about using the firehouse they had already conveniently fixed to douse the fire. It was a fight to bring the flames under control but they were able to keep them in check until the arrival of the near-by fire brigade. The police had also arrived and Superintendent Hamblin of 'B' Division placed a cordon of police around the area. Colonel Majendie, Colonel Ford and Captain Shaw were 'early on the spot' and quickly began interviewing key personnel already on site. Photographs were taken from 'different view points' and an artist's eyes and skills were brought to bear on the wrecked scene. The Police and the Explosives Department had become practised in the art of dealing with explosion situations.[49]

Whilst the officials had to wait upon more extensive searches, analysis and deliberations before giving a formal conclusion, the press were lucky in finding an expert already on the scene. By amazing coincidence, Major Bagot just happened to be passing along Victoria Street, when he heard the explosion and hurried to give help. He had some experience of explosive materials, and brought it to bear on the scene of the crime as he set about gathering data. As he entered the Booking Hall, he registered the distinctive smell of dynamite. He knew the authorities would want to know what type of explosive had been used so he set about obtaining the means to carry out a test. Unable to acquire some lignic acid, 'he tried the effect of vitiated atmosphere on an ordinary razor' which, despite the delay, 'was sufficiently conclusive to his mind' that it was indeed dynamite. He noted that the greatest degree of damage had been done laterally, proven by the bulging walls, at precisely the same height as where the explosive material must have been. He further noted that 'the supports of the roof, not the roof itself that [had given] way, whereas laterally objects much further distanced than the roof had been literally pulverised'. He also noted that the subway from the District Station to the termini of the London, Brighton & South Coast had its iron rails broken and twisted into 'the most grotesque shapes'; the stairwell was filled with masonry from above, but little damage had been done to the subway itself despite the bomb exploding right above it.[50]

Captain Shaw's initial summation and report to the Metropolitan Board of Works merely stated the facts and gave no conclusions:

Called at 1.30 am (Tuesday) to the Victoria Station, Buckingham-palace road, Pimlico, to the premises of London, Brighton and South Coast Railway company (J P Knight general manager) cause of occurrence unknown; contents and building insured in the Liverpool and London and Globe.

Damage – cloakroom of one floor 30 by 30ft., and the contents destroyed by explosion and fire, booking office and refreshment rooms adjoining and contents seriously damaged by explosion. William Ford, aged 27 years, and Karl Katten, aged 29 years, injured and taken to hospital. Adjoining damages – the premises of the London, Chatham and Dover Railway.

Company (Mr Harris, manager) roof damaged by fire and breakage and window glass broken; the premises of the Metropolitan District Railway Company (Limited) (Lord S A Cecil, general manager) window glass broken; and Nos. 1, 2, and 3 Victoria-buildings occupied respectively by Messrs Baker & Co., tea merchants and F Fernando, chemist, window glass broken and contents damaged by dirt.

Once the fire was out, a thorough search was made of the debris under the watchful eye of the experts. Evidence was soon unearthed, including a clock spring (which proved a valuable link), and bits of metal perhaps from a tin. As the search continued, it became clear that the bomb had emanated from the left-luggage cloakroom. The cloakroom porter remembered a man leaving a leather portmanteau, which was very heavy, and asking the porter to be 'very careful with it'. In the light of this, searches were made in other stations.

'The Infernal Machine' as it was named by the newspapers of the time. Happily this one failed to function. It was found by stationmaster William Hart in a search of one of the cloak rooms (luggage) on Paddington Station in 1884. In 1937, the *Great Western Railway Magazine* wrote of it, 'It is the back view of an American-made clock to which a pistol is attached by wire, and a second wire passes through the handle grip from which the woodwork had been removed and connects it to the movement. The clock when discovered was embedded in dynamite weighing 22 lbs., and packed around it were a number of iron bullets. The pistol was loaded and cocked for firing … it was intended that the trigger would gradually be pulled as the wheels of the clock revolved, a cartridge would then be fired, the dynamite exploded, and Paddington Station might have been blown sky high.' It is believed that this was the type of bomb that exploded in Victoria Station. These metal pieces were also found inside the portmanteau. They would have become lethal missiles in the explosion – the penny is to give an indication of size.

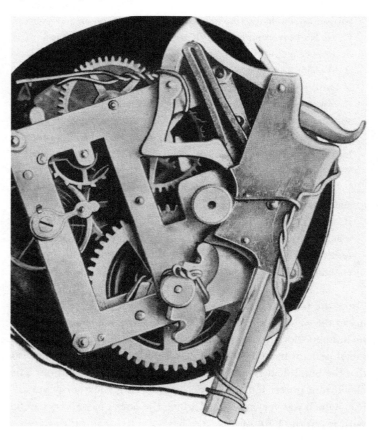

Pieces of iron forming part of the charge from the infernal machine.
Note.—The penny is included to show the relative sizes of the bullets.

On the following evening, Wednesday 27 February, a black leather portmanteau, which had been deposited in the cloakroom of the South Eastern Railway's Charing Cross Station, was discovered. Then, on Thursday afternoon, a small brown leather bag, which had been left in the early evening of the previous Monday (25 February)· was found at Great Western Railway's Paddington – both contained an 'infernal machine'. It turned out that the Charing Cross bag had already been deposited at least once before.

In his evidence to the court, Major Majendie described the contents of the Charing Cross bag. He had found forty-five cakes of 'Atlas Powder A' – all marked the same and all wrapped in the same kind of paper. He explained that Atlas Powder A is a form of dynamite in which wood pulp is substituted for the usual absorbent *kieselguhr*; it is exploded by a detonator in the same way as ordinary dynamite. Atlas Powder A was not a licensed preparation in Britain and had no commercial use here; it was manufactured at a chemical factory in Philadelphia. (Analysis showed that it contained almost 72.5 per cent purified nitroglycerine.) *The Times* called the slabs 'an engine of destruction of a very formidable nature'. The slabs were packed around a tin box which contained part of a clock with a portion of pistol, attached with copper wires, which were fastened to parts of the clock that would not impede the working. The pistol was a Remington or an imitation of such. There were seven detonators in one slab, with their mouths presented to the muzzle of the pistol. It had been set to go off at 12 midnight, and the hammer had fallen on the cartridge but it had failed to explode. There was a loaded bullet in the pistol, of a type made by the Union Metallic Cartridge Company, Bridgeport, Connecticut, USA. He confirmed that he had found substantially the same contents and set-up in the bag from Paddington Station, except that the tin box was of a cash box type.

Yet another such bag was found on Saturday morning, by John Langley, cloakroom porter of the London, Chatham & Dover Railway at Ludgate Hill. This luggage room was close to the stairs where thousands of passengers passed every day. Langley found a portmanteau of the same size and 'character' as those already found. On opening it, the stationmaster, Mr Bowman, found yet another 'infernal machine', again comprising a pistol attached to a clock and cakes of the American Atlas Powder. Two American-produced handkerchiefs and old American newspapers were stuffed around to keep it in position. The bag and its contents were taken by the city police to Old Jewry Police Station and Colonel Majendie was sent for. The brave colonel then proceeded to defuse the bomb, taking care to 'separate the pieces prepared with fulminate of mercury from the cakes of dynamite'. There were a total of forty-seven cakes about 'the size and thickness of a man's outstretched palm and fingers', making a total weight of 25lb. The reason it had not exploded was, again, because of a failure of the trigger mechanism. If it had, the paper made a point of saying, it would have killed not just a great many English persons, but also many 'Irish-labouring classes who use this station for cheap rides to the third station out – the Elephant and Castle – … where a large number of them congregate'. This was followed by further searches at other stations but nothing else was found. Colonel Majendie called for 'more searching and unwearied examination by the police … for a great crime has beyond all doubt been planned and attempted and the terrible and intended consequences of this crime have only been escaped by a slender chain of what it would be profane to call "accidents"'. [51]

Through painstaking investigations of previous incidents, under-cover infiltrations and inside informants, the Special Irish Branch and City police already knew that this was part of a Fenian cam-paign, and had a good idea who the individuals involved in these railway bomb attempts were. They knew where they had come from (America), how and when they had arrived (Southampton and Liverpool), their names, and under which aliases they might be operating, and generally where they might be in hiding. The Home Office offered a princely award of £1,000, which the four railways involved – the Great Western, the South Eastern, the London & Brighton and the London, Chatham & Dover – promptly doubled. Descriptions of the four American Dynamitards were given.

John Daley (otherwise Denman, or Norman) was apprehended at Birkenhead Station, preparing to travel to Wolverhampton. Upon being searched he was found to have two packets of explosives and an 'infernal machine' hidden in his clothes. James Francis Egan, Daley's landlord at Crafton Road, Sparkbrook, Birmingham, was also arrested and charged with 'conspiracy to cause an explosion in the United Kingdom likely to endanger life or case serious damage to prop-erty'.[52] The other two being sought were Harry Burton and James Gilbert Cunningham, who were not caught until sometime later.

A 'Criminal Outrage by Enemies of Order'

The year 1885 started with a bang – and then many more of them. Saturday 25 January became known as 'Dynamite Saturday' as the Fenians attempted to blow up a number of locations around London, including London Bridge, the White Tower of the Tower of London, and the House of Commons.

On 2 January, an explosion occurred, once again, on the Underground. It was of a different nature to those that had taken place previously. It was indeed the work of a different team of Dynamitards.

The local Hammersmith train left Aldgate four minutes late at 8.57 p.m. The train, as described by Joseph Hammond, the guard on duty that day, consisted of:

... a break-van at the rear, in which I [Hammond] was, and there was
an engine and six carriages – Harry Taylor was under-guard, he was
next the engine – there was a break compartment and a third-class
carriage next the engine, then two more third-class with what we call
spear-breaks in each, then a first-class, then a composite carriage partly
first and partly second class, and I rode in the rear as guard in charge –
we allow passengers to ride in the spear-break with the merchandise.

It is the second third-class carriage that is of significance, and in
particular, the 'spear break van'[53] in the first compartment. It was
here that several witnesses said they saw James Cunningham and at
least one other man. Whilst it was usual for the guards to ride in
these break vans, it was not unusual for passengers to also ride along
with the passengers' luggage when the train was full, or, when passengers were trying to get on as the train was moving out of the
station (a not uncommon occurrence, that and getting off before it
stopped). There are four stations between Aldgate and King's Cross:
Bishopsgate, Moorgate, Aldersgate Street and Farringdon Street,
after which comes King's Cross, then Gower Street. Between the last
two is the Charlton signal box, and it was at roughly 9.14 p.m., some
150 yards west of the box that a 'violent explosion' occurred, and a
sheet of flame lit up the tunnel. So violent was it, that it smashed
thirty-two windows on the train and put out all of its lights. Above
the ground, the effects were also dramatic causing 'persons crossing
the Euston Road in close proximity to the gratings [to be] thrown
off their feet' and horses [pulling vehicles] having to be strongly
restrained to stop them from running away. Back down below the
gas lights at Kings Cross and Gower Street Station were blown out
and, at the latter, several women waiting on the platform fainted.[54]
The train came slowly into Gower Street, whereupon the under
guard called, 'All change' and the passengers got off. Amazingly, apart
from 'fright' or 'shock' there were only minor injuries sustained.

The train was taken on to Edgware Road for inspection, and the
authorities were soon on the scene – Mr Godsden, Chief Inspector
of the Metropolitan railway, Superintendent Williamson of Scotland
Yard, Superintendent Harris of 'S' Division, Superintendent

Thomson of 'E' Division, and Inspectors Wells, Kelly and Livingstone. Investigations showed that the tunnel wall on the northern side had been struck – presumably by something that had been thrown from the train travelling to the city – some 1½ft above the ground, leaving an indentation of some inches deep for about 2ft, and some ballast had been thrown about. It was not believed to be gunpowder, as none of the tunnel walls were blackened, but rather the smoke of the previous twenty years had been cleared. Other than that there was little damage done to the tunnel.

The total effect was very local. The Hammersmith train was on the southern side going westward, but a train on the northern side passed the damaged train briefly lighting up the horrendous scene. Most reports said that the explosion came from the front of the train. Colonel Majendie believed it to be a 'percussion bomb' (such as that used in the assassination of the Emperor of Russia), and that the explosive was contained in an earthenware ball as, if it had been glass, there would have been some remaining evidence no matter how small the crystals.

Good gathering of evidence from passengers and railway employees, identified that James Cunningham was in the spear break van in the second carriage, before the train started and when it drew into Gower Street. People also stated that a man had gone aboard with a package and come off without it. Perhaps the most damning evidence was that of John Seward, Hyde Park Constable 11, who stated that he had, not only seen Cunningham in the van, but Cunningham had leaned out of the window and asked him for a light or a match. He had also seen a 'workman's flag basket on the seat' similar to those carried by railway employees for their tools. Another policeman, Sergeant E42, Michael Crawford, stated that he had seen three men inside the spear break van, standing talking when it stopped opposite the ticket collector's box by the stairs. He had been distracted by a lady who was bleeding from the nose, and they had made their exit. He confirmed that one of them was Cunningham. (It was believed that Burton was one of the others.)[55]

In May 1885, James Gilbert Cunningham and Harry Burton (believed to be the mastermind behind the 1884/5 London

The explosion that happened at Aldersgate Street Station was the work of 'person or persons unknown'. It is believed that an 'anarchist' set 'the bomb' with a time fuse in the first-class carriage at the previous station – Farringdon Street. When the bomb exploded one man was mortally wounded and he, Harry Pitts, became the first terrorist death on British railways.

bombing campaign) were charged, tried and found guilty of the lesser charge of 'Treason Felony – Act of 1848', (this did not carry the death penalty, rather than 'High Treason' which did), in respect of the explosions in London; in particular the White Tower at the Tower of London, the Victoria Station explosion, the one at Gower Street Underground, and of the conspiracy in relation to the bombs at Charing Cross, Paddington and Ludgate Street stations. Both men declared their innocence. They were sentenced to 'penal servitude for life'.[56]

First Terrorist Death on the Railways

Whilst the Fenians' campaign had effectively been brought to a standstill by mid-1885, the anarchists were getting into their stride. Dynamite was their weapon of choice also. There were many anarchist groups known to the police and the Intelligence Service. The Autonomie Club in Windmill Street was one, which was linked to the 'Martin Bourdin Affair'.

On 16 February 1894, Bourdin, a believed anarchist of French origin, took 'the South Eastern Railway ... from Charing Cross to Greenwich, [he] no doubt jostled against many worthy citizens at the ticket office or on the platform and sat side by side with them in the railway carriage.'[57] He did all this whilst carrying a volatile explosive device. So volatile, that he blew himself up in front of the Royal Observatory with the bomb he had carried to the park, thereby creating enormous speculation. What was his intention? Was he an anarchist bomber? Why was he carrying an explosive substance? Was it a tragic accident or did he truly die 'for the Revolution'? No one truly knows. The anarchist press described the explosives expert, Col Majendie's, assumption that Bourdin intended to blow up 'the Observatory, its contents, or inmates', as 'utterly absurd' and it is interesting that Bourdin was not claimed by the anarchists as a martyr to the cause. In fact, they wanted to distance themselves from the whole affair.'[58] This whole episode is another 'unknown' in the dynamite conspiracies of that era.

Rollo Richards, however, was an anarchist. He declared himself to be one. He was born in 1861 in Clapham, so was a local man. He was a member of his local 'Educational Society' – a euphemism for anarchist group. He was not a man in the first heady rush of youth. In August 1894, when he started to wage war against 'the Establishment' and planted a series of bombs to blow up Post Office property, he was, in fact, thirty-three years old. Somehow, he evaded capture and was not apprehended for these 'felonies' until early March 1897. When eventually arrested, he was found by the police to be somewhat eccentric and rather strange, given to 'wild, obscene language'. He was also found to have bomb-making apparatus in his room.

In April, he was tried at the Old Bailey for causing an explosion by gunpowder likely to endanger life, found guilty and sentenced to seven years penal servitude.[59] All this is significant because it is believed that the bombing of Aldersgate Street Station was in retaliation for Rollo Richards' harsh sentence. It is even more significant because it led to the first terrorist death on the Underground.

The 1880s had been the decade of the 'Dynamite Campaign' on London's railway stations and the Underground. It had created havoc, fear and injury, but had not yet brought about death. All that was to change on the evening of Monday 26 April 1897, when the unsuspecting men and women of London were making their way home from work via Aldersgate Street Station.[60] The station was not one of the original seven stations when the Underground opened in 1863, but was added when the Metropolitan Underground line was extended out from Farringdon Street. Aldersgate Street Station opened in 1865, on the site of 134 Aldersgate Street which, at one time, had a building that bore a sign boasting, 'This was Shakespeare's house'. Whilst a Subsidy Roll (records of taxation) from 1589 shows that *a* William Shakespeare was indeed the owner of the property, there is nothing to indicate that it was *the* William Shakespeare, famous playwright.

Dastardly Outrage on a London Train

BOMB EXPLODED IN A CARRIAGE

ONE MAN KILLED
NINE INJURED.[61]

If we disregarded the first word, dastardly, the headline could relate to happenings in recent living memory. This headline, however, relates to an incident at Aldersgate Street Station in an earlier century.

Why Aldersgate Street Station? Well, it was an extremely busy station because it had four sets of rails which were used by a number of companies: the Metropolitan District, the Great Western Railway, Great Northern, the Midland, and London, Chatham & Dover. It was

also a terminus for local trains. It is, however, apparent from the findings, that it was not the station itself that was targeted, but rather one
of the trains that passed through the station, although one is left with
the feeling that some thought went into the choice of this station in
particular. The layout of the station meant that an explosion here, or
in its approach tunnels, could create enormous chaos, confusion and
damage, not just to one train but to several others – and so it proved.
The Metropolitan train on which the bomb was planted was 'blown
to pieces' and a London, Chatham & Dover Company train, standing across the platform on the southern side, was 'badly wrecked'.[62]
In the immediate aftermath, escaping, panicking passengers could
easily have been mowed down by other trains entering the station,
as a 'down-train' was indeed about to do, as they clambered and
crossed the numerous rails seeking safety on the other side. Whoever
had planned this 'dastardly outrage' was obviously familiar with the
Underground, and certainly achieved the mischief and mayhem
intended – although maybe not as much as they had hoped for.

The train was proceeding eastward around the 'Circle' from
Farringdon Street and was, therefore, on the northern side of the
station at around 7.10 p.m., a time when passenger traffic was particularly heavy. The explosion occurred in the centre compartment
of a first-class carriage as the train drew up at the platform in the
station. It blew out the gas lamps on the Metropolitan side, plunging
the station into semi-darkness. A report in *Lloyds Weekly Newspaper*,
2 May 1897, gives a graphic description of the scene:

> The wrecked carriage, still attached in its original position to the
> train, looked a remarkable object. The roof and sides of the carriage
> had completely disappeared; but the body of the carriage was secure,
> though badly damaged. The aperture made in the centre of the com-
> partment was V-shaped, the upper part being the widest. The flooring
> in the centre presented a huge hole, blackened and jagged at the edges.
> It was nearly round, and was about three yards in circumference. The
> case of one of the ceiling lamps of one of the wrecked compartments
> was all that was left by the explosion, the force of which had hurled it
> upwards, but, still adhering to the gas-pipe which runs along the roof

of the coaches, it had fallen over the off side of the next compartment, where it remained suspended at a level with the window strap. The glass in the train was wrecked, while the adjoining metals [track] were strewn with woodwork and debris.

Such was the force of the explosion that timber from the carriage was hurled upwards and became embedded in the roof of the station some fifty feet above. Station Master Dow, interviewed immediately after the event by a member of the Press, was able to give an early eye-witness account:

'I was standing just here (by the bookstall on the central platform). Just as the train drew up I was sensible of a terrific explosion. My first impression was that something had come through the glass roof, for it was the splintering of glass which I first understood. Then all was confusion. Passengers came out from the carriages screaming.'[63]

It is rather an understatement, as other first-hand reports show:

There was a deafening report and a flash, which is described as being like the explosion of a small mine ... [it] created an indescribable scene of wreck and alarm ...

Some of the glass from the roof commenced to fall with alarming noise, and crashed onto the platforms, staircases and metals ... glass panels in the doorways and passages of the station were blown to pieces ... portions of the wrecked carriage being hurled across the station ... several passengers being similarly treated ...

... the sufferers lying about the station, in various positions, cut and maimed in various ways. One man's leg looked as if it had been shattered, and other persons were bleeding from various parts of the body.[64]

Another company employee, the ticket examiner, described his experience of the explosion, 'It seemed as if I was lifted upwards several times and dropped violently on the ground ... I don't want another sensation like it.'[65] The noise was such that it was 'heard in Farringdon Street Station on the east and Moorgate Street Station on the west and inquiries were instantly wired through as to what had occurred.'[66]

Upon learning the circumstances, railway officials and City police, headed by Superintendent Mackenzie, soon arrived, the latter with 'street ambulances with them'. Nobody was in the carriage. The platform, however, was full of people waiting unsuspectingly to board the train, and many were injured, from flying timber, glass and other carriage debris, at least ten severely and one mortally.[67]

The following is a list of those who were reported injured and taken off to St Bartholomew's Hospital by ambulance or cab:

William Hall, aged 22, of 3 Cambridge Street, Hyde Park
Paul Geogi, 35, of 27 Shepherd's Bush Road
Sarah Ship, aged 50, C Block, Polygon Buildings, Clarendon Square, St Pancras
William Daniel, 33, of 30 Abdale Road, Shepherd's Bush
Arthur Spawforth, 33, of 94 Fordwych Road, Brondesbury
Theophilus Trustrum, 35, of 17 Albert Road, Forest Lane, Stratford
Mr Nelson, of 12, Portland Terrace, St. John's Wood
Arthur Washtell, 14, of 29 Stanmore Street, Caledonian Road
Simon Israel, 22, of 22 Latimer Street, Stepney
The first seven mentioned were admitted as in-patients.[68]

A plain clothes City police officer, Police Constable 801, John Sutton, was on duty at the station at the time of the explosion. He was also injured, suffering cuts to his right leg and left thumb. Like the others, he was transported to St Bartholomew's Hospital for treatment, then to the City Police Hospital in Bishopsgate Street.[69]

The poor man whose leg was shattered was to make it into the record books as 'the first death on the Underground caused by a terrorist bomb'. Harry Pitts had been quickly transferred to the hospital, but died of his injuries around 11 p.m. that night. Pitts was born in Devon on 27 June 1861, the son of a millwright, but at the time of his death was residing at 31 Wickham Road, Coleraine Park, Tottenham. He was foreman for Mr F. Ayres' Aldersgate Street firm, and he left behind a wife and three children. Later, a fund was raised by his company and its employees to assist his family. (The jury of the inquest also donated their fees and made a subscription towards the fund.)[70] His brother identified his body at the inquest, which opened on 30 April and was immediately postponed until the representatives of the government's Explosive Department had finished their examinations of the train (which had been moved to a siding at Moorgate Street Station) and could be present.

So, what exactly happened? Well, in truth, no one knows exactly, since no one was ever apprehended for this crime and no confession were ever made. The first immediate thought was that there had been an accident, probably caused by the explosion of the gas cylinder, which provided gas for lighting. This was now located not on top but under the carriage; however, the stationmaster reported that there had not been any particular smell, and certainly not that of gas. Further examination showed that the gas cylinder was still intact, but did have an indentation from the outside, where something had exerted great pressure upon it. Examination by Colonel Sir Vivian Majendie, Her Majesty's Chief Inspector of Explosives, and his assistant Captain Thomson, showed that the explosion had spent the major thrust of its force in a downward direction, rather than spreading longitudinally and upwards.

It would appear that Majendie is referring to the detonation wave here, not the expanding gases. Both would occur with a detonation. When a stick of explosives is ignited the detonation progresses from the detonator end, down or along the stick. If the stick(s) were laying on their side the progression would be longitudinal and, because it was on the floor, the easiest direction for the gases would be upwards. If the sticks were standing upright then the progression would be down the sticks of dynamite (assuming the detonator was at the top). This would give a downward thrust. In either case, the gases generated would have to expand, throwing debris in a hemisphere and hence hitting passengers on the platform.

When the inquest into the death of Henry (Harry) Pitts was resumed at the City Mortuary on Monday 24 May, several witnesses gave evidence. Joseph Howard, the driver of the train, told the court that it had 'resembled the discharge of a cannon, followed by a cloud of splinters, wood, glass, dust and smoke'. He was complimented by the coroner on his 'presence of mind in sounding his whistle to stop another approaching train the moment the accident happened'. This action had probably saved a great many lives.[71] Police Constable Larker, who had aided Pitts, reported that he had found him 'lying on the platform ... opposite the shattered carriage'.[72]

Dr Calverly, who had care of the nine wounded who were admitted into hospital, informed the court that there was no metal present in any of the wounds.

The last and 'most important witness' was Colonel Majendie, who had, by now, considerable experience with bombs on the Underground. He gave his verdict that 'the explosion was not due to gas or steam' but rather 'a high explosive' and that this 'was not in a metal case', but that it had been 'ignited on the floor of the carriage'. This was the fourth Underground explosion, the main difference being that this was effected in the train itself and set alight by a fuse. James Hardy, the head guard, corroborated this when he reported that 'as they were coming out of Farringdon Street station a porter called out that there was smoke coming out of one of the carriages'.[73] The porter was one C.S. Martin, whose statement was reported in *The Times*:

> As the 6.59 train was leaving the station ... he noticed smoke coming from a first class compartment. He opened the door and tried to pull the mat out as he thought it was on fire, but owing to the increasing speed of the train he failed to do so. He called out to the rear guard ... [but] he was unable to see the cause of the smoke.[74]

A 'modern-day' Majendie suggests a possible scenario:

> It is probable that the dynamite used for the bomb was fired using safety fuse. This is a cord with a black powder (gun powder) core that burns at a steady rate. At that time production was a bit haphazard so a user would normally take say a foot or better a yard and light it. He would then time the burn rate to hence calculate how long a fuse was needed for the time delay required. The made up bomb would have a few 8oz sticks of dynamite, a plane detonator (blind tube, probably aluminium or copper but if improvised it could be any tube

that was closed at one end) with the safety fuse crimped into the detonator. To fire the bomb it would be lit using a match, or maybe a cigar, and placed into the carriage. The burning mat would then be lit by the dropped match (or cigar) or from the burning safety fuse (think modern Chinese firework delay fuse but a lot longer and larger diameter).

Colonel Majendie concluded that this was 'an outrage of formidable character and the most despicable nature'. The jury returned a verdict that 'Pitts had met his death … by a bomb or some other explosive maliciously placed in the carriage by person or persons unknown' and, the coroner summed up, '… that amounts to wilful murder'.[75]

All information was passed to Inspector Melville of the Criminal Investigation department who proceeded to make further inquiries into 'the mysterious occurrence.' Despite the efforts of the railway and police authorities no one was ever arrested, let alone tried for this murder. It has remained 'person or persons unknown'.

DISASTER

HEXTHORPE – A RACE DAY 'SPECIAL'

The railways brought many, and some surprising, new opportunities. Once Thomas Cook had started his famous 'excursions' with his Temperance group in July 1841, the scene was set for group or mass travel to a particular destination. The *Illustrated London News*, of September 1850, writes, 'One of the most prominent social characteristics of the present time is the growth and progress of pleasure-travelling among the people ... The great lines of railways of England, by granting facilities for 'monster' or excursion trains at cheap rates, have conferred a boon upon the public ...'

Unhappily, along with the 'boon' of cheap tickets came a price of a different kind. *The Saturday Review*, 8 August 1863, reflected that, 'As soon as ever the excursion trains begin to run plentifully, the accidents follow in like proportion ... the railway accident season has begun ...'

Racing, the sport of kings, was also a popular fancy for the lower and middle classes, and thousands had followed the horses at meetings all over the country for centuries. The railways were quick to seize the opportunity for a new source of revenue, and laid on 'specials' not just for the human fans, but also for the equine participants. Tolson and Vamplew tell us, in their work, *Derailed: Railways and Horse-Racing Revisited*, that the 'Liverpool & Manchester Railway were operating excursions to Newton races in June 1831 less than a year after its opening' and:

At Doncaster the railways demonstrated how one company – The Great Northern Railway – with only one modest main line station could co-ordinate the activities of up to eight companies so expertly that between 1848 and 1908 it handled an increase from about 8,000 racegoers to 190,000 in some 350 trains on St Leger Day alone. By suspending almost all freight traffic over its system and clearing up to seventy miles of sidings in the vicinity of Doncaster, the GNR was able to despatch a train every seventy-five seconds using just one regular passenger station and a couple of temporary locations.[1]

Doncaster's Gold Cup is the oldest significant flat race in horse racing in Britain, and 'Cup Day' is the highlight of Doncaster Race Week. On Friday 16 September 1887, a Midland Railway's Race Week 'Special' was one of the aforementioned 'monster' excursion trains. Pulled by engine No. 1588, a six wheel coupled engine with tender, the train consisted of 'brake van; one bogie third-class; one composite; two bogie composites; one bogie third-class carriage; and a bogie third-class brake carriage; or twelve passenger vehicles, considered with the bogie carriages to be the equal of a

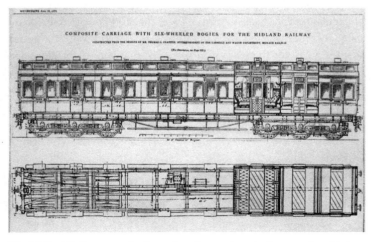

The Midland Railway were the first to introduce twelve wheeler upgrades of their third-class carriages, introducing bogies for better running and safety; however, most of the injured in the Hexthorpe accident were in third-class carriages.

train with seventeen vehicles!'[2] (Bogies had been introduced by the Midland in 1874.[3] The bogie, a pivoted framework, holding four or six wheels, enabled a greater body length and could allow the negation of sharper curves. They also gave a smoother, more comfortable ride and had a better safety factor than the old fixed-wheel carriage which would more easily leave the track.)

The Midland excursion train was packed – even overloaded – with almost 1,000 race goers, all looking for a great day out. It left Sheffield at 11.20 a.m. as a 'Race Special', and stopped for the collection of tickets at Hexthorpe ticket platform at 12.13 p.m. Two minutes later, the 11.20 a.m. train found fame for all the wrong reasons. [4]

Hexthorpe ticket platform was not one intended for alighting from or boarding a train, it was just for ticket collecting – a neat way of ensuring everyone had paid, and expediting entrance into the racecourse. The platform was merely a short, narrow, wooden structure, with a meadow on one side and the South Yorkshire line on the other. It was 1½ miles (2.4km) west of Doncaster, in the area known as Hexthorpe Flatts, just on the Doncaster side of the road bridge. The platform was situated on the Doncaster-bound line, and was used only for the collection of tickets, particularly on the days of excursions for Doncaster Race Week. Nobody in the train, or on the platform, expected anything untoward. It was business as usual, as it had been for the past seven years, but that was to change when the stationary excursion train was smashed into by the 8.40 a.m. Manchester, Sheffield & Lincolnshire Railway (MS&L) daily express train travelling from Liverpool to Hull.

In the words of the *Illustrated London News* (24 September), who ran a large and detailed account and carried a graphic depiction of the scene:

The Manchester, Sheffield, and Lincolnshire Company's train had nothing to do with the races; it carried many persons for Doncaster, but was a regular daily train, and was going on to Hull. In the ordinary way, the driver of this train would not stop at Hexthorpe ticket-platform; and the driver in charge of the engine was a man of considerable experience, who knew the train well; he belongs to Liverpool, and his name is Taylor … his train, nevertheless, rushed on at high speed, and struck the end of the Midland Company's train with such momentum that the collision was a terrific force. The wood-work of the carriages was smashed and splintered as if the wood of a packing-case; the massive iron tires and frames and wheels were twisted into fantastic forms. The screeching of the escaping steam from the partially

All of the drama and horror of the smashed train and traumatised passengers is captured in this depiction from the *Illustrated London News*.

broken engine mingled with the agonising screams of the unfortunate people imprisoned by the wreck of the carriages, and with the groans of many who had sustained dreadful injuries. For a while, discipline seemed lost and reason suspended amongst officials and escaped passengers alike; but the panic did not last long; the work of succour and rescue was commenced, and within an hour nearly fifty persons were extricated and placed on the platform and in the adjoining sheds for the mineral traffic on the line, where they received prompt attention at the hands of surgeons and physicians.

Incredibly, there were five doctors travelling in the express train and so medical help of some kind was immediately available. They worked as best they could, using horsehair stuffing from the torn and ripped seating to staunch bleeding wounds, and wood from the broken carriages as splints and stretchers. Others soon arrived, from Doncaster Infirmary, and more sophisticated procedures, such as amputations, were conducted on site. Sergeant Escexetz (? several spellings around of this), of Hexthorpe, was close by and saw the collision. He rushed to help and officiate, and found a nightmare of the first order, horrifying, hellish, and to make matters worse, it had started to rain. The sergeant found that there were already several dead, so he arrested the driver and the fireman of the MS&L train for manslaughter.

Reporting the Accident

Hexthorpe was one of the most serious accidents in the history of the railways up to that time. The media of the day – local and national newspapers, weekly and monthly magazines, in all parts of the country (and indeed in several parts of the world such as America and Australia) – covered the story of the accident in great detail; leaving nothing to the imagination, rather providing every last aspect possible. In the days without our modern media networks they saw it as their job to 'paint the picture' and 'record the words', so that the general public would miss nothing (and, of course, they would increase their sales). Their graphic descriptions would seem more than over the top in today's reportage, but then we can easily resort to visual images, whilst they, like Charles Dickens, needed to provide words to conjure up the images that their readers readily devoured. The papers were also determined, and happy, to highlight the terrible cost that had been paid by the ordinary people because of the railway companies' obstinacy, recalcitrance, or even greed.

On Saturday 17 September, the day after the accident, under the headline, TERRIBLE RAILWAY ACCIDENT NEAR DONCASTER, *The Leeds Mercury* carried a three and a half column intensive report, giving a blow-by-blow account of the accident and its painful consequences. It gave factual information:

> The last carriage of the train [the Midland excursion] was a bogie composite consisting of a guard's van and several passenger compartments. Into this vehicle the engine telescoped as far as the boiler dome losing its funnel, and rising more than a foot from the front wheels …
>
> It is a remarkable fact that none of the carriages [of the MS&L express train] left the rails and the permanent way was not at all damaged …
>
> About forty or fifty yards of the ticket platform was ripped away by the carriage doors flying open, and fifty yards of the handrail at the back of the platform was broken by the smashed framework of the vehicles.

It then goes on to paint the casualty scene with virtually every groan, gouge, decapitation and disembowelment covered:

> Another painful incident and one which afforded, if one was necessary, proof of a mother's love, was that of a woman who had evidently been carrying her child in her arms. When the shock occurred she must have folded it to her breast to shield it from harm, for when found the child was dead, suffocated by the pressure whilst the mother was almost decapitated … In another carriage was found a man suspended by the neck from the two hat racks which had been driven together like a vice.

The *Illustrated London News* painted the scene in somewhat broader, but still powerful brushstrokes, whilst, a few days later the *Lloyd Weekly Newspaper*[5] blazed the atmospheric headline, 'AN EXPRESS DASHING INTO AN EXCURSION TRAIN', with the following:

> The result of the collision was that the guard's box was smashed nearly to atoms, but the guard being engaged in collecting tickets, escaped with his life. The last passenger carriage was telescoped over the next and this and the succeeding carriage were broken to splinters … The scene presented a moment after the collision will never be forgotten by those who saw it.

Then it provides lines and lines of gruesome and heartbreaking detail. It has to be said that the papers did a thorough job in bringing the reality of the horror and the human price of the accident to the public at large.

All the reports wrote about the state and appearance of the carriages, how they had been 'smashed to pieces', 'broken to splinters', 'just like matchwood' and 'telescoped'. Carriages in those days were, of course, constructed mostly from woods chosen for their differing appearances, strengths and costs. The Midland had been through a programme of replacing all their old carriages with new stock from their new Carriage and Wagon works in Derby, and this programme was virtually completed by mid-1886. John Pendleton wrote, in his iconic work, *Our Railways: Their Origin, Development, Incident and Romance*, 'The Midland Company were the first to discover that the third-class passenger was the life and soul of the English railway, and they have reaped the most benefit from accommodating him.' They had already begun carrying third-class passengers on all trains from 1 April 1872, but from what was to be an historic day, 1 January 1875, they dispensed with the second class and replaced it with a much improved third class. They later introduced upholstered and buttoned seats stuffed with horsehair, and more leg room. Such radical action was looked upon with great scepticism and anger by other companies, some of whom even called it a 'revolution'. (Ironically it was the MS&L that were the first to copy the Midland's lead in this.)

Despite this upgrade, the carriages that were most affected in the accident were the lower class. Wood, broken under pressure, collapses, shatters, pinions and pierces, making it a lethal component in a situation like Hexthorpe. Perhaps the one small consolation was that these carriages were still oil-lit and not lit by gas, because leaking gas added to the danger of explosions in later collisions.

Eyewitness accounts filled many inches of the numerous columns, from passengers on both trains and from the railway employees. The witnesses expressed shock, relief, incredulity, but little apparent anger. That came later.

One eyewitness, who actually saw the accident in motion, was local Hexthorpe resident, Mrs Osborne. She was in her bedroom which overlooked the sidings, and she watched the excursion train draw up and stop at the platform. Then she heard a great crash and saw the engine of the Hull express ploughing into the back carriages of the stationary train:

> One coach, the vehicle forming the tail end of the train, appeared to have simply been wiped out, and the locomotive had forced its way into the other, losing in its thrust the funnel and piercing the woodwork up to the cylinder. The end of the engine, a part of its buffer had broken by the impact, had gone right into one carriage and buried itself half way up to the driving wheel.[6]

Mrs Osborne gathered up some things and rushed to the site to help. What she noticed in particular, and what struck her as 'remarkable' was the fact that 'most of the sufferers had their clothes torn to shreds.' The sights and sounds she saw and heard would have challenged those with the very strongest nerves, yet it is reported that, 'the medical gentlemen speak highly of a lady [Mrs Osborne] whom they described … as working with mingled energy and calmness in the midst of a scene which recalled the horrors of a battlefield.'[7]

The Dead

Descriptions and information about the dead featured large in most of the reports. A list of persons, whose dead bodies were removed from the train and carried to the mineral sheds at Hexthorpe a short distance from the scene, appeared in the *Leeds Mercury* on Monday 18 September 1887 (and also appeared in several other papers over a number of days). Sixteen probably died instantaneously and were found dead, whilst three more succumbed to their injuries a short time after the collision, before being extricated from the wreckage. Amongst the dead at the scene were a husband and wife, and a mother and her toddler son. Five others, who had been transported as quickly as possible to Doncaster Infirmary, died later over the following days, bringing the number of husbands and wives to three, and the total number of people killed to twenty-five. The lists of the dead and injured stated name, age, occupation, address, marital status and number of children – all of which provide insight into their status and background:

Mrs Mary Alice Fillingham (33), 139 St Mary's Road Sheffield

Frederick Lee (19), ivory cutter, Field Head Road, Sheffield, unmarried

William Hardy (42), foreman warehouseman, 131 Broomhall Street, Sheffield

Mrs Mary Mitchell (24), Carlisle Street, Sheffield

Thomas Bradbury (36), printer, 55 Randall Street, Sheffield, married, six children

George Rodgers (41), saw file maker, Lansdowne Road, Sheffield, married, five children

Jane Rodgers (40), wife of the above

Harold Russell (22), saw maker, Dorset Street, Sheffield, married

Jane Halle (38), wife of Charles Thomas Halle, (police constable, Sheffield, amongst the injured)

Susannah Beaumont, wife of James William Beaumont, Theatre Tavern, Arundel Street, Sheffield. Her husband died later at the Infirmary. [They left two children]

Edward Dougherty (72), Arundel Street, Sheffield, married

Frederick Thorpe (28), file grinder, 13 Grapes Yard, Lock Street, Infirmary Road, Sheffield, married

Elizabeth Middleton (35), wife of Henry Middleton (carter), George Street, Sheffield

Walter Middleton (12 months), son of above

Frank Kirkland (22), pearl and ivory fluter, Pearl Street, Sheffield, married, one child

Frederick Calow/Charlow (38), electroplater, Wellington Street, Sheffield. (His wife, Mary Calow, so badly mutilated that it took a long time to identify her, later died at the Infirmary). Two children, the younger, (eight months old) escaped the accident without injury

James Moxley Swift (35), printer, Fitzwilliam Street, Sheffield, married

Henry Barnsley (31), tobacconist, Crown Street, Wellington, Salop, married, two children

Arthur Mitchell (29), son of a farmer, Brightside Farm, Sheffield (husband of the above Mary Mitchell).

Those who came to the dead looking for family or friends found them laid out in a row with only faces exposed, the rest covered with sacking to hide bodies grotesquely mutilated and sometimes dismembered. Husbands or wives, mothers and fathers, even friends had the painful duty of trying to find their loved and dear ones amongst the row of grossly damaged bodies. Several, such as the man whose 'head had been fearfully smashed, his face crushed beyond recognition' and was also 'disembowelled', were only identifiable by their clothes or other articles upon them. Not surprisingly, this man was the last to be identified and was eventually named as Arthur Mitchell (29) by his brother.[8]

The five who died later in the Infirmary were identified in news reports as: Mrs Annie Durley; Henry White (65), 31 Lansdowne Road, Sheffield, who lived with his son, who had come to him in the Infirmary, and was with him when he died; Mrs Mary Burley (46), whose husband had visited the previous evening; and Daniel Hawkesworth, of 91 Lendmills Road, was reported to have 'died at half-past eleven [on Sunday 18 September] after suffering great pain', which brought the number of deaths to twenty-four.[9]

Addy Thompson (46), of George Lane, Sheffield, was the last to die, on Wednesday 5 October, bringing the final count to twenty-five.

One of the human interest stories features four of the dead, who worked for the printers Spalding & Co. in Sheffield, all in the same shop. Edward Doherty, William Swift and John Henry Quip were all compositors, and Thomas Bradbury was the foreman lithographer. They had obtained 'leave of absence' to go to the races for a fun day out, all mates together. Their fun was short lived, as the first three died at the scene, whilst Quip died the following day. They all left families. Thomas Bradbury had borrowed a sovereign from another friend but had not told his wife about his trip, and neither had the others. Their family and friends only realised something was wrong when they failed to return home as usual in the evening. They then discovered the 'jolly' and had to identify the bodies for the inquest.

The Injured

The number of reported injured increased day on day. First forty, then seventy were reported and, finally, ninety persons were reported as having been injured. It was surmised by the press that there were probably more, not badly hurt and able to get away under their own steam and anxious not to be identified because they were taking an 'illegal' day off and did not want to jeopardise their situations at work. Some of the injured, thirty-one in all, were on the MS&L train, including the two guards. The head guard, travelling in the third vehicle from the front, was so unwell that he had to be interviewed at home in his bed. As the numbers of injured grew, the Infirmary struggled to contain and deal with the patients that were arriving by the cab-load, minute by minute. News had travelled fast, and locals came forward to offer their own homes to assist. Seven of the injured were treated at the Reindeer Hotel and six initially in private homes – nos 15 and 7 Young Street, and no. 35 Cartwright Street. Later that evening, these were stretchered to the Reindeer Hotel, where qualified nurses were in attendance to care for them, having been transported in by train from London by 9 p.m., to

boost the Infirmary's inadequate nursing numbers. Amongst those
reported as initially remaining in private houses in nearby Balby and
Hexthorpe were:

Jonathan Sanderson – Lydgate Crooks, near Sheffield; one broken leg
Austin Simmonite – 158 Alexander Road, Henley near Sheffield;
both legs broken
Mrs Connelly – Britannia Inn, Lambert Street, Sheffield; broken leg
and badly injured
George Savage – 25 Ashford Road, Sheffield; broken thigh, large flesh
wound and generally bruised
Emily Savage (wife of George Savage), Sheffield; broken leg and seri-
ously injured in various parts of the body
Jnno (?) Love (40) – Well Lane, Wath; broken leg and bruises
Hannah Aston (38) – 12 Church Street, Wath; injured arm and bruises
J.H. Baggeley – Hedge Bank, Sheffield; sent home as he was able to walk
Mrs Harisson – Pearl Street, Sheffield; general bruises and shock to
the system.

One wonders how these home owners with good hearts felt, having to
face this burden of responsibility in their bedrooms or front parlours.

A further list of the injured was written up in the *Birmingham
Daily Post*, Monday 19 September 1887:

Anthony Fitzpatrick – near Eastwood, Notts; fracture of rib and
injury to the lung (also reported with concussion of the spine by the
Leeds Mercury)
John Denton – 97 Werditou Street, Kentish Town, London; concussion of the spine
Maggie Foster – Eyre Street, Sheffield; concussion of the spine and
bad wound on the leg.

Amongst them were those who had 'concussion of the spine'.
Concussion of the spine was a railway accident phenomenon. It had
become so common that it was part of the legal, medical, assurance
and even social vocabulary of the day, not just in Britain but in many

countries across the world. Right from early accidents, and over the following decades, it excited and challenged the minds of the medical profession so much that a plethora of books and articles were produced in Britain, America and Europe. John Eric Erichsen became one of the first experts in this new field. His first full length medical study of the condition, 'On Railway and Other Injuries of the Nervous System', was published in Philadelphia in 1867. It became a 'classic', the reference point for all of the opinions and theories that came after; for this reason, 'railway spine' is often known as 'Erichsen's disease'. The exact nature of 'railway spine' was hotly debated, some medics taking the stance that it was definitely a physical injury – a trauma of one type or another to the spine itself. Others argued the greater importance of the psychological aspects, believing 'hysteria' played a larger role. There was a third view, however, held by those who were more sceptical (particularly those who argued on behalf of the defendant railway companies). They maintained that the condition was not a condition at all but purely a deceitful way to claim compensation. In his book, *Railway Injuries with Special Reference to Those of the Back and Nervous System and Their Medico-legal and Clinical Aspects* (to give its full title), Dr Herbert W. Page, who held the office of Surgeon to the London & North Western Company for seventeen years, is sceptical. He based both his books (the previous one, *Injuries of the Spine and Spinal Cord and nervous Shock*, Churchill, 2nd edn, 1885) on his experiences, and case studies over five years. He cites Thorburn (another expert), 'in the case of railway accidents … the general public of this country has been educated to expect 'concussion of the spine' with paralysis, and that, in the minds of the laity, the very mention of a railway accident calls up the required idea'.[10]

Railway injuries became a medical 'speciality' and 'appearing for the plaintiff' became an integral part of being a doctor treating railway accident patients. *The Lancet* medical journal carried many articles to educate, advise and assist the physicians and surgeons of the day. These covered topics such as 'Compensation for Railway Accidents', F.C. Skey, FRCS (6 Sept 1862, Vol. 80), 'Railway Accidents and Railway Surgeons', J. Jones (9 July 1864, Vol. 84) and 'On Cases of Injury From Railway Accidents: Their Influence Upon the Nervous System, and Results', Thomas Buzzard, MD (13 April 1867, Vol. 89). Further articles continued at regular intervals.

What is most apparent from the lists of injured from Hexthorpe is that the majority are suffering from leg traumas, many extremely serious, and many that turn out to be life-affecting, even life-changing injuries:

Tom Trimnell, solicitor, London: compound fracture of one leg, with amputation, and with a bad wound on the other, in a bad way

Addy Thompson (36), George Lane, Sheffield: compound fracture of one leg and simple fracture of the other

William Stokes, 112 Pond Street, Sheffield: bad fractures of one leg, simple fracture of the other

Thomas Marples, Duke Street Park, Sheffield: simple fracture of the legs

William Rodgers – 23 Harewood Street, Sheffield: amputated leg and simple fracture of the other

Alfred Fordin, 84 St Mary's Road, Sheffield: compound fractures of both legs

Henry Jarvis, Artisan View, Henley: simple fracture of both legs, fracture of one rib, scalp wounds

William Jarvis: two simple fractures of both legs

Henry Bocking, Red House, Parkgate, Sheffield: compound fracture of one leg

John Conselly, Britannia Inn: compound fracture of one leg

Thomas H. Vernon, Union Street, Sheffield: compound fractures of both legs, left one amputated

Frederick Wm Rogerson, 164 Thomas Street, Sheffield: compound fracture of one leg and simple fracture of the other

John Goldsmith, Royal Oak Inn, Sheffield: compound fracture of one leg, simple fracture of the other

Ada Barnes: bad compound fracture of one leg (amputation probable) and injury to the spine

Anna Stokes, 121 Pond Street, Sheffield: fracture of the thigh

Mary Ann Stokes, 121 Pond Street, Sheffield: fracture of the thigh

Annie Durley, 277 Shoreham street, Sheffield: (a girl of thirteen years old whose mother was killed) fracture of the thigh and scalp wound

John Loach, Jubilees Villa, Albert Road, Handsworth, Birmingham:
fractured collar-bone and much bruised
Jarvis Kay, Sheffield: bruised leg
Samuel Lovell, Sheffield: fractured legs
Charles Hale, police constable, Sheffield: internal injuries and wounds
at the back of the right leg
George Ackham, Sheffield: fractured leg
Michael Wood, Wormwell: fractured ribs.

Such injuries are not surprising, as bone breakage or fracture is
the usual outcome of severe impact or intensive pressure and these
bodies had experienced both – from the train and from each other.

Compensation

It was obvious from the outset, even to the MS&L Directors, that
there would be a great number of claims for compensation. The
company immediately acknowledged that it would not dispute lia-
bility, and that all who met the company 'in a just spirit will be dealt
with quickly and satisfactorily'.

The men employed by the MS&L also realised that the
disaster would cost the company dearly, maybe too dearly –
job-cutting dearly! More than five hundred hands were employed
at Mexborough, a major railway junction, where, on Sunday
25 September, Mr Richards the stationmaster, called a meeting just
days after the accident. Such was the strength of feeling that the
chiefs of the locomotive, goods traffic and permanent way departments attended, along with over 300 men. The purpose of the
meeting was to discuss proposals put forward as to how best 'help' the
company, and show the shareholders and directors that they, the men,
sympathised and wished to help them with 'the loss they had sustained'. It would, the men hoped, 'cement the unity already existing
between employers and employed as had not been witnessed on any
other railway in the Kingdom.'[11] What the men proposed is extraordinary, especially when one remembers that railwaymen were not

amongst the well-paid workers of the time, and especially when one remembers that their chairman was known for his high-handedness and being tight-fisted. There were three proposals: 'that every man should give two days' pay; that each man should give a week's pay (each to be distributed over a period of three months); and third, that everyone earning above 23s a week should give a week's wage and those earning under to give three days.'[12] The second proposal was carried by a large majority. Following this, another meeting was held a few days later, this time mostly fitters, blacksmiths and labourers. These 150 gentlemen were filled with 'a good deal of indignation' and stated they 'would not submit any part of their wages for such a purpose'.[13] A Special Meeting of the Board of Directors was held on Tuesday 4 October 1887, to receive a deputation of the men from all grades. Sir Edward Watkin spoke for the Board, expressing their full appreciation and stating that the offer would amount to at least £6,000 and could even reach £12,000.[14] He declined, saying that the Board could not 'allow those who lived by the sweat of their brow to tax themselves for such a purpose'.[15]

The cases for compensation were heard in many different localities, since several of the victims were not local to Sheffield or Derby, and they took many months, even years, (into 1889) to complete. A great many were reported in the papers. Here are a few, to give an impression of the nature of the claims and how they were dealt with.

A Sheriff's Court was held at the Law Society's Rooms in Sheffield, on Friday 1 June 1888, to assess the damages payable to two casualties. The first, notable for the life affecting injuries and for the amount of compensation, was Mr Thomas Trimnell, a young man of twenty-seven years of age. Trimnell was a solicitor, and it was reported that he had made a good start in business, had been successful and doing well but that it would be at least another year before he would be able to do any further professional work.[16] The matter of his income was important in the equation for compensation and, being a 'professional man', his would be a much more substantial claim than most of the other victims.

Mr Trimnell was a first-class passenger in a carriage in the rear of the train – the first carriage to feel the full impact of the collision.

The compartment in which he travelled was extensively crushed, and he was very severely injured when his left foot went through the floor of the carriage and was virtually severed from his leg. It could not be saved and was later amputated. His other leg was also severely smashed but saved by the skill of the surgeon, although it would not be of use for some time as it frequently broke out with consequential abscesses and ulcers about the wounds.

Prior to the accident, Trimnell had been of previous good health, describing himself as 'very fit ... a good athlete', but in the months following the accident he had been in great pain and 'nervous distress'. Giving evidence himself, Trimnell told the Court:

> There was a tremendous smash ... I was jerked upwards and hit the hat rail ... Then the carriage telescoped ... the roof gave way and the flooring gave way ... I was sitting in the left-hand corner facing the engine, the right-hand portion of the compartment telescoped completely, fortunately my end didn't ... my legs were fixed in the material above the bogie engine ... railway officials broke part of the carriage and extricated me ... I was taken away leaning on the shoulders of two men. I noticed that my left heel was in front and my toes behind, my foot hanging on by a small piece of skin ... I was attended on the embankment by a doctor and was one of the first taken to Doncaster Infirmary.

Mr James Smith, the surgeon who had treated Trimnell at the Infirmary, said he had not seen the plaintiff since he left hospital but that he found him 'much deteriorated, more emaciated'. It was obvious to all that the young man was in a very poor way and finally the Under-Sherriff advised the jury that the case had been put in a 'very fair way ... without exaggeration' and to 'use their own good sense and give the plaintiff a fair and reasonable sum'. After just a fifteen minute deliberation, they awarded Trimnell £4,000 in damages. (£4,000 would be roughly £350,000 now.)

The same jury was also involved in assessing the case of Arthur Forster, a commercial traveller in the employ of Messrs Earl & Son, iron and steel merchants. His left leg suffered a 'comminuted fracture' whereby the bones of the leg were broken into small pieces. At the time of the hearing the bones were not all healed and 'there was a gap in the bones'. He had been treated first at the Infirmary, and then taken to Reindeer Hotel to be nursed, where he had remained until 28 November, for the most part confined to bed. Like Trimnell, Forster claimed he had suffered a 'severe shock to the system ... from which he still suffered.'[17] Forster was claiming for his 'medical attendances, loss of earnings, expenses, cab fares, etc., totalling £373 6s. The jury awarded him a more generous sum of £950.'[18]

Mrs Carey, a small shopkeeper of Peterborough, had her case heard at Huntingdon where she was awarded £550 for her injuries.[19]

Another held a good distance away, was one in the Middlesex Sherriff's Court. Here, on 18 December 1887, before Mr Under-Sherriff Burchell and a 'common jury,' stood Mr Henry J. Leeman, and his brother William Leeman, both fishmongers of Bishopgate Street. Under the direction of the Under-Sherriff and with the defendant company (the MS&L) allowing judgement to go by default, the jury awarded Mr Henry Leeman £200.[20] For Mr William Leeman, however, it was a slightly more contentious situation and he had brought two medical men, Dr Brendon and Dr Gibbon, to give expert opinions on his behalf. William Leeman told the jury that, being in Sheffield at the time, he had decided to visit the races and so he took a third-class ticket on the ill-fated train. He further informed them that fourteen persons in the same compartment had been killed outright, whilst he had been thrown from his seat and had then to make his escape through the window. At the time he did not think himself severely injured, and went to the assistance of several other passengers but, the sight of seeing three people having 'their legs cut off and their wounds dressed'[21] made him need to leave the place quickly, and he returned to Sheffield and thence back to London. Back home he found himself experiencing bouts of great excitement and great anger against the company. He consulted Dr Bredon in Norton Folgate, explaining he was having dizziness, nervousness and 'a want of sleep'. Dr Bredon sought a second opinion and this doctor advised 'a change of air'. Taking this advice, Leeman had incurred expenses in being 'driven around the country' and visiting Brighton in an attempt to improve his health; however, he was still suffering from 'great nervous prostration' and complained of the effects of the accident. Called to give evidence, Dr Gibbon proffered the opinion that, 'it was no use giving patients suffering from nervousness arising out of railway accidents any drugs, but the best thing to do was to advise them to be in the open air as much as possible and give them a "bromide of potassium" in order to induce sleep.'[22]

The disorder discussed here as 'nervousness prostration' and some-times also identified as 'hysteria' or simply 'shock', is what would now be diagnosed as post-traumatic stress. Like 'spinal concussion' this condition, under its various names, became one of the major discourses in railway accidents. Herbert Page covers it extensively under the title, 'The Fright Neuroses', which he prefers to the more common 'traumatic hysteria'. He confesses that despite 'naming' the disorder, the medical profession are little more forward in understanding 'what is the precise morbid change underlying the so-called functional disorders of the nervous system ...' Again he cites Thorburn, this time, interestingly with regard to his observations of a woman involved in the Hexthorpe accident:

> ... a case of a woman with left hemianaesthesia [numbness of the whole left side] following severe shock and bruises in the Hexthorpe collision .... her mental condition was remarkable. She had an intensely frightened 'scared' look like that of a wild animal. She paid little or no attention to her surroundings and it was with the greatest difficulty that she could be got to answer even simple questions. She was quite incapable of connected speech, but there were none of the emotional manifestations usually regarded as hysterical ... there was for a time a profound mental change also of hysterical origin. A year later the condition had passed.

Leeman's Counsel argued that, because of his 'nervousness', he was greatly out of pocket, having had to hire in a buyer to go to market, and from the falling off of his business since he was unable to conduct it fully. This amounted to about £6 a week. The defendant's counsel argued that the claim was excessive and, finally, the jury assessed the damage to be in the region of £100. Interestingly, Leeman had had the foresight to insure himself when buying his travel ticket, and so also received 25s from the Passengers Assurance Company, as compensation for the injuries he had received as a result of the accident.

On 7 July 1888, the *Manchester Courier and Lancashire General Advertiser* reported two further cases of compensation settlement. One William Stokes, whose leg injury necessitated amputation, accepted £1,400 and Henry Bocking, publican, who had had a compound fracture of the leg, accepted £800. The paper reported that 'there now remain only three claims, all of them, however, for substantial amounts'.

Most Serious

One of the three cases that probably expected 'substantial amounts' was held in Sheffield, in October 1888, before the Under-Sherriff and jury. Thomas Henry Vernon (43), married with three children, was a successful businessman, a cork manufacturer, with a business he had taken over from his father. Vernon had lived a very active life before the accident. Immediately after the collision, he 'came to' at the bottom of the embankment with blood streaming down his face and he could not raise his left arm at all. Trauma to his left leg was so severe that it had to be amputated and, thirteen months later, his right one was still useless. He also suffered from memory loss and 'feeble action of the heart'. His prospects for improvement were poor. The jury awarded 'heavy damages' of £4,500 – the largest amount given,[23] although this was later reduced to £4,000 on appeal by the MS&L.

The last claim for compensation, dealt with some twenty months later in June 1889, was a big case with seven medical gentlemen appearing as witnesses or to assist counsel, this was not counting the MS&L Company's own Chief Medical Officer, Dr Thorburn. Several railway companies kept medical men on the payroll, mostly to deal with compensations claims. G. Neele, superintendent of the London & North Western Railway, wrote, in his *Railway Reminiscences*, that although the company had medical practitioners who covered different districts, it was '… decided to have one consultative man for the whole line, and Dr Annesley ... was selected. Subsequently a special 'Medical Committee' was organised, at which passenger claims of a serious character, or beyond the limit of my free action, were dealt with, and the Medical Officer attended as adviser.'

Mr S.D. Waddy, QC, appearing for the plaintiff, Mr Frederick William Rogerson, suggested that the jury, upon hearing the evidence, would come to the conclusion that this was 'the most serious of all cases arising from the accident' because the injuries were 'not only far reaching, but of a permanent character and last as long as he lived, and in all probability they would shorten his life.'[24] Frederick William Rogerson was young (it was estimated he was born 1858 or 1859, so probably thirty years old) and had previously been 'vigorous and active in every way', but was now 'a cripple for life'. He had been apprenticed to his father as an edge tool forger at seventeen years old and, before he was twenty, had saved £100. This was important information in determining his loss of earnings or potential income as no 'books' or receipts of any kind had been kept in regard to his earnings before the accident.

Rogerson reported to the jury that he had been 'excessively thrown' around the carriage during the collision, ending up with his head out of the carriage and his legs still inside. He remembered that he had to ask people to 'hold his right foot'. He spent fourteen weeks in the Infirmary but requested to go home for Christmas, since when he had experienced 'violent palpitations', which he attributed to his heart. He had never had anything like that before. That Rogerson had a 'disease of the heart' was corroborated by his several medical experts. That the disease was brought on by the accident was fiercely disputed by the defence. They also disputed his evidence of a substantial income of some £200 per year, finding it 'not proven'. The jury obviously found the same, because they finally awarded him just £1,500.

The amount of costs incurred by the MS&L in pay outs amounted to many thousands of pounds. On Thursday 27 December 1888, *The Sheffield Local Register* (from *The Sheffield & Rotherham Independent*) had a list of damages awarded, although it was not complete:

Annie Burley, aged 14   £550

5 children of Mr and Mrs J.W. Beaumont, an annuity each of 10s a week

14 May

Miss Foster   £350

Mr Bell   £425

1 June

Mr Thomas Trimnell   £4,000

Mr A. Foster   £960

30 June

Mr W. Stokes   £1,400

Mr W. Bocking   £800

10 July

Mr and Mrs C. Sharpe   £1,150

10 August

Mr Henry Redfern   £350

16 October

Mr T.R. Vernon   £4,500 (Reduced 14 November to £4,000)

Leaving aside the children's annuity that amounts to £13,985. Others found are:

Charles Dobson   £270

Henry Jarvis   £500

Mr H. Leeman   £200

Mr W. Leeman   £100

Mrs Carey   £500

Mr W. Rogerson   £1,500

This amounts to £3,070, making a total of £17,055. That, however, was not the whole story. This is only a fraction of those injured, to say nothing of the compensation for the twenty-five deaths. The final sum would have been a staggering amount.

Inquiry and Trial

On Monday 19 September, Major Francis Arthur Marindin, RE, CMG, member of the Railway Inspectorate since 1875, arrived to carry out an Inquiry on behalf of the Board of Trade. He immediately proceeded to the scene of the accident to inspect the site which had been, as much as possible, left as it was. Such was the demand for admission that he had to set up his inquiry in an alternative location to that planned at the MS&L Railway offices. He moved to the room where the Local Board of Guardians held their meetings. Here, he interviewed officials from both railway companies, as well as all of the other employees involved – some twenty-five, including Mr Halmshaw, district superintendent.

Halmshaw told Marindin that the 'absolute block system' had been operational on the line since September 1880 – with the exception of Leger and Cup race days. On such days the system was suspended by the Great Northern Railway, and so was not in operation on the section of the line between Hexthorpe Junction and the South Yorkshire Junction (a good distance of 1 mile and 28 chains). He produced a copy of the notice given to drivers regarding operational instructions for these special days. It was the same year on year. The 'permissive' system of controlling the line had been used each time with no problem. The 'flag signalmen', who were used during these particular periods, were given special instructions to keep the red flag up the whole time there was a train at Hexthorpe platform. (Unfortunately the guard charged with this duty was stood in such a position he could not actually see Hexthorpe platform.) The men in the signal boxes were told not to lower their danger signals until speed had been reduced. He also informed Marindin that, on that Cup Day, twenty-five trains had been dealt with between 9 a.m. and the time of the accident – approximately 12.15 p.m. (roughly one every four minutes – although the MS&L train was only two minutes behind the Midland train).

The invention of the 'telegraph' had brought better safety possibilities to the railways, including the 'block system'. The 'absolute block system' was a method of working the trains on the track under the supervision of the signalmen in the signal boxes, who used the telegraph to communicate from one box to the next. Previous to this, the trains were controlled within blocks on a 'time' system – five minutes allowed between trains – but this had been open to all sorts of mishaps and misinterpretations. The telegraph came into being in the early half of the nineteenth century but was initially expensive and complicated. After further development, and much government coercion via the Board of Trade, it was taken up and used by a good percentage of the railway companies, but not enough of them, so it was finally made compulsory by Parliament in 1889 (after the notorious Armagh accident, in which a Sunday school excursion train's brakes failed and eighty people were killed and some 260 injured). The concept was simple. The track, whether single, double or multiple, was divided up into sections or 'blocks' between two signal boxes, and at any one time only one train should be inside a block. If there was only one train in a block, then there would not be any collisions. A train could not enter a block unless the one ahead was empty. The signalmen on either side would control this. This was the theory, and, putting aside signal failure or human error, in the main it worked very effectively; however, the 'absolute block system' had one drawback: it was time-costly. It was too costly on race days, and so, rather than introduce extra signal boxes to speed things up, even though the track would be under more pressure from higher usage, and despite the fact that resorting back to using 'flagmen' introduced a greater possibility of human error, the block system was suspended between Cherry Tree box and South Yorkshire box on Wednesdays and Fridays during Doncaster Race week.

John Mason, driver of the ill-fated Midland excursion train, gave evidence that, although he had been given no specific instructions, he had simply followed the danger and flag signals, reduced his speed and, when the train already at the platform had moved away, he had approached the platform and stopped at around 12.13 p.m. He was stationary at the platform for approximately two minutes before his train was hit. The first jolt of the collision did not move the engine at all, but the second moved it some 20 yards forward. He went to the rear of his train to see what had happened, and found the brake and three bogie carriages severely damaged, whilst the remaining carriages were hardly touched. He saw, he said, that the engine of the MS&L's express train (a Sacre 4-4-0 locomotive) was fine, with steam blowing off at ordinary pressure (this description is somewhat at odds with that of eyewitness, Mrs Osborne, and the report by Major Marindin). The Inquiry continued all day, and was then suspended until the following afternoon so that the Major could attend the coroner's court in the morning. By Tuesday 20 September, he had finished his enquiry and was able to give evidence at the coroner's court on that same day.

The coroner had sat on the case on several occasions. Initially, and immediately, to identify those already dead at the scene of the accident, and thereafter to identify those who died subsequently. A further sitting was required to determine if there was a case to answer. Major Marindin believed there was, his feeling being that the block system should not have been suspended – 'if [it] is necessary as a safeguard under the ordinary conditions of service, it is surely all the more necessary when the number of train is largely increased ... the alternative arrangements were not all that they could have been.' Whilst he acknowledged that the driver had 'lost no time in applying the continuous brake, sanding the rails, sounding the whistle and reversing the engine, doing all in his power to stop his train', he concluded that both the driver and the fireman of the MS&L train were at fault for not obeying the signals given, and he said so in his report.[25]

Samuel Taylor (39), of 21 Whally Street, Toxteth Park, Liverpool, and driver of the fateful train, was an experienced driver. He had worked for the MS&L for twenty years. His fireman, Robert Davis (28), of 25 Nelson Street, had worked for them for eight years. Davis confessed that he had seen a guard with a red flag, who had also held up his hand with one finger up (sometimes a finger was held up and moved around to start a train). Not understanding what the guard meant he had not informed his driver. The driver believed that he had responded to the signalman's instruction – the Hexthorpe Junction starting signal was off (but had a red flag under it). He had reduced his speed and proceeded cautiously; however, the curve and the bridge over the line obstructed the driver's view, and it was not until he was on the bend that he had sight of the stationary train, at which point he had reacted immediately.

At the coroner's court, the men were represented by Mr W. Warren and Mr Warren Jr, solicitors, of Leeds, who had been retained by their union. It was the first time a union had taken such an action. Thursday 22 September 1887 was not an auspicious day for Taylor and Davis. The Doncaster Borough coroner resumed his inquiry following the jury's visit to the site of the accident. After hearing further testimony, the coroner outlined his understanding of the evidence, stating that, 'the signalling had been carried out most faithfully',[26] but neither the driver nor the fireman had looked out for them. He directed the jury that, if the arrangements that the company had set in order had been followed, no collision would have occurred. After such emphatic direction the jury brought a verdict of 'guilty of manslaughter'. The coroner issued a warrant for the pair's arrest. He agreed bail on a surety each of 50*s*, but, not having the money upon them, they were taken into custody. Later that day they appeared before the Magistrates' Court and were formally charged. They were bailed on the same conditions and sureties as before, as offered by T.G. Sunter, secretary of Associated Society of Locomotive Engineers and Firemen, and C.E. Stretton, vice-president of Amalgamated Society of Railway Servants.

The verdict was not popular amongst the general public, who thought the wrong persons had been put in the dock. A letter, which appeared in the *Liverpool Mercury* on Saturday 24 September 1887, summed up the general feelings:

> The people who are not only morally but actually to blame are the directors and managers of the line, who suspended the block system for the two heaviest days' work in the year, at a time when its services were imperative … It is time the farce of punishing workmen for the faults of the directors was brought to a close and the real guilty persons convicted. If a few directors were to be locked up for a smash like Hexthorpe we should soon hear of measures being taken which would prevent their reoccurrence.

On Sunday 25 September, a number of experts, deputised by the Amalgamated Society of Railway Servants, tried to visit the site to gather information in preparation for the trial. They were denied access to the track.

The trial of Taylor and Davies, for 'the manslaughter of Mrs Jane Hale and other persons killed in the accident' was ground-breaking in the railway world. It made legal history, and was an outstanding event in the history of the Society.[27] Held at York Castle on Wednesday 16 November 1887, it excited a great deal of attention and curiosity, and large numbers attended the proceedings. The prosecutor's case rested on the 'culpable negligence' of both men in either not looking for the flag signals, or not responding to them. The defence found themselves facing all the custom and prejudice which had proved so hard on drivers in similar accidents in the earlier history of railways.[28] The defence's case was two-pronged: a) that the signalman and guards had failed in their duty, having given contradictory directives – this they proved through robust questioning of the men involved; and, b) that the type of brake (the simple vacuum brake) in use on the train was totally inadequate.

Brakes

Having spent a great deal of time, ingenuity and effort in getting locomotives and trains moving, it seems unthinkable today that no thought was given to the need to be able to stop them when required or the consequences if they could not (as was witnessed by the tragic death of William Huskisson). O.S. Nock writes, 'while engineers vied with one another to increase the tractive capacity and the speed of the locomotives, no-one in those early days made any attempt to develop the science of braking'.[29] Even when the need for brakes was conceded, the 'Battle of the Brakes' raged long and bitter in the British railway world for decades. Lined up on one side were the railway companies (and their shareholders), and on the other side were the Railway Department of the Board of Trade and the public.

Brakes began to be fitted to some carriages, usually the first class because they tended to be the heavier. These were worked by a 'brakes-man' who was sat on the roof, leaping (at his peril) from wagon or carriage as and when braking was required. 'In the 1850s the practice of fitting out a "brake-van" at the end of the train began',[30] but the matter of what brake, where and how, was unresolved. There had been deliberations, discussions and even trials (1875, 1876 and 1878[31]) of a number of different types of brakes – chain, hydraulic, handbrake, vacuum, automatic compressed air – and numerous warnings and recommendations by the Board of Trade. They were only recommendations because, with existing companies, the Board of Trade was still totally impotent to enforce anything.[32]

In Sir Edward Watkin, the MS&L Railway had a chairman who was mindful of the purse-strings under his control, and to whom his first loyalties lay – and they were not to the public or his employees, but rather to his company and shareholders. Under Watkins' managerial hand, the MS&L had adopted Smith's simple vacuum brake. It was a decision that was to cost the public and railway servants dearly. The simple vacuum brake, when not in use and with the power off, remained at atmospheric pressure through the train. To apply the brakes the driver had to put the brake handle into a position to create a vacuum, this required a steam jet in the ejector, evacuating the air from the brake pipe system of the entire train. All this obviously took time – vital time that meant the difference between crashing, death or damage, and stopping.

The MS&L were no strangers to calamitous railway accidents. By the time of the Hexthorpe disaster they had, in their recent past, already experienced three dreadful incidents at or near Penistone, in 1884, 1885 and 1886. The latter was greatly exacerbated by the use of the simple vacuum brake, resulting in twenty-four dead and over sixty injured. At that time, Major Marindin yet again reported for the Board of Trade. One can imagine his exasperation when he said:

> The value of a brake having, above all, automatic action can hardly be contested and although the Board of Trade has, as yet, no power to insist upon the adoption of a continuous brake possessing these quali-

ties; yet I would remind the Manchester, Sheffield and Lincolnshire
Railway that this is the second emphatic warning which has been
given to them.[33]

Ironically, the Midland had also used Smith's simple vacuum
brake and found it reliable, but, of course, it wasn't automatic. It
tried a number of systems but, after the Wennington accident of
1880, it made an effort to equip its passenger trains with the automatic vacuum brake and this was completed by 1883, though some
engines continued to have the Westinghouse automatic brake until
the mid-1890s.[34]

In his summing up, Lord Chief Justice Coleridge, presid-
ing, directed the jury that, before they convicted the prisoners of
manslaughter, they would have to say whether they were guilty of
culpable negligence because they misunderstood two contradictory
orders. Wanton disregard of duty had to be proved before negligence
could amount to criminality; however, if they were found culpable,
the prisoners should not go unpunished. The jury deliberated for
just half an hour. The foreman of the jury gave their verdict – 'not
guilty considering the contributory negligence of the guards, the
absence of cord communication, and the conflicting nature of the
signals.'[35] The prisoners were discharged.

Such was the elation amongst drivers and firemen nationwide, at
this historic win, that 2,000 members of the society signed a letter
of appreciation to the 'legal and professional gentlemen engaged in
the defence'.

The cost of the trial and defence was over £295, but, as reported in
their next annual report, ASLEF was more than satisfied, 'We feel we
have been amply repaid, for we secured the acquittal of our members,
and a large influx of members has been our reward. The books show
an increase of 474 members, in addition to seven new branches opened
in the year.' They were not the only ones overjoyed. The drivers and
firemen of the MS&L also wrote an effusive letter to the solicitor:

We no sooner saw them put in fetters than one and all we rushed to
their relief, and at once sought your powerful aid to release them, and

fortunate indeed were we to find that your able services were at our disposal. We are proud to congratulate you upon the valiant manner in which you conducted them through the ordeal through which they had to pass, and brought them out scatheless, and by so doing brought joy and happiness back again to those homes and families which to all outward appearance had been almost forlorn and destitute. Never, therefore, can we forget the great sympathy you evinced towards them, and the indefatigable zeal you displayed to bring about so glorious and successful an issue.

Hexthorpe was to prove one disaster too many for the MS&L Railway in hanging onto their preferred brake system, especially after the Lord Chief Justice, in his summing up at the end of the trial, commented, 'I cannot but think that the railway company was seriously to blame for having had in use a brake which not only was not the best in existence, but which was known to be insufficient and liable to breakdown.' Such was the public indignation and hostility towards the company that, shortly after the close of the trial, the decision was taken to change to the automatic vacuum brake.

Ironically for the more 'caring' Midland Railway Company, Hexthorpe was the worst disaster to befall a Midland train, and to make matters worse, it was through no fault of their own. Hexthorpe was tragic for many reasons, not least because the outcome of only a few seconds of human confusion was a tragedy of gothic proportions.

THE TAY BRIDGE
DISASTER

Tay Bridge – famous, notorious, second only to London Bridge. Both calamitous, both known for falling down. In the 'Tay Bridge Disaster', as it is always called, it is the bridge that captures the attention and is the focus of discussion or examination. It has intrigued and exercised many great minds since that calamitous night in 1879. It has become the stuff of myth and legend, even whilst it is subjected to every new technological and scientific analysis that becomes available. Numerous articles, notable books, engineering papers and reproductions have been published yet, even today, there is dissent and controversy over the various theories that have been put forward as to why the bridge came down – and with it a train load of innocent people, who, until comparatively recently, were something of an afterthought in the grand debate.

What makes this such a dark and devastating event, one that stands out amongst the many truly dreadful railway catastrophes, is that no one survived. Not one. It was a total violation, biblical in stature. Even the Board of Trade regarded it as, 'removed out of the ordinary category of railway accidents.'[1] It overwhelmed everyone. Not just locally or nationally but all around the world, people were aghast. It shook society, stunned railway people and startled engineers into examining their responsibility in such matters. Did they carry a collective responsibility here? 'Its fall is beyond any question in some way a reproach to the engineering science of Great Britain,' wrote *The Engineer*. Were they, as a profession, remiss in not having guidelines and suggestions for allowances to be made in differing circumstances, and for varying materials to resist wind pressure? Such questions were raised by the press, in engineering and architectural journals, and at the Court of Inquiry.

Undoubtedly, the bridge deserves such attention. It was an iconic achievement in a brave new industrial age. It won its designer, Thomas Bouch, a knighthood bestowed by a Queen 'graciously pleased'. At the time of its completion it was boasted to be the longest bridge in the world – some even claimed it to be the Eighth Wonder of the World, or at the very least, a wonder of its age. *The British Architect* journal wrote that it was, 'regarded as one of the greatest engineering feats that the world has ever seen accomplished.'[2] Whilst others, even at that early stage, doubted its integrity. It is said that Sir John Fowler, designer of the Forth Bridge, would not let any member of his family across the bridge, whilst many local businesses would send their mail and their coal, but not themselves, across it.

Bridges are described and explained by: a) their design – it was a lattice girder design; b) their length – almost 2 miles (3.2km) long with eighty-five spans of varying widths; and c) their materials – combining cast and wrought iron. Nothing awesome in that, it may seem. Yet, awesome it was to prove, then and even now. It was awesome in its audacity, in its perspective and its construction.

Resident civil engineer, and manager of the Tay Bridge contract, Albert Grothe, writing in the monthly periodical *Good Words* in 1878, tells how it was decided to:

> …dispense with the staging and scaffolding which are generally used in bridge building. The piers and girders were to be erected on shore, and floated out to their destination. The consistency with which this principle was carried out would distinguish this bridge from all other structures of the same kind, even if its size and importance were less remarkable. No matter of what material the parts were constructed, whether they were iron receptacles for concrete, huge lumps of brickwork weighing above two hundred tons, or iron girders of one

hundred and ninety tons, they were all finished on shore and floated to their destination. [3]

However, it is not that straightforward, and this is not quite the actuality, as Allan Rodgers explains:

> This is an interesting quote for it gives the clear impression of a bridge largely built onshore, with its completed parts simply floated out and placed on site. The reality was markedly different, as a reading of Grothe's full article would show. The bridge was a complex structure, whose design had to be radically altered after the initial construction of the first few brick piers on the south side showed, all too clearly, that the assumed solid bed of rock was just not there. The design of the piers and their foundations differed from place to place and the girder spans differed in width and length and each of these differences necessitated variations in the methods adopted to construct them on site.
>
> Undoubtedly pioneering and innovative construction methods were used for the building of the re-designed structure with its cast iron columns instead of brick piers. Parts of the structure, such as the large iron caissons for the concrete and brick pier foundations and the wrought iron bridge girders, were indeed built onshore and floated out to site. The iron bridge piers, however, were not. Although the individual column sections were cast in the foundry at Wormit, the completed piers, with their columns and cross-bracing, were built in-situ, out in the river, as was all of the brickwork above sea level.

'Light, 'graceful', 'airy', and 'narrow like a ribbon' (it was only 14ft 10in wide),[4] even 'fragile', are some of the descriptions that appeared in the press. Ulysses S. Grant (18th President of the USA), who stopped by for a visit on 1 September 1877 during his World Tour, is reported to have called it, 'A big bridge for a small city'.

It was a bridge that carried big ambitions for the North British Railway who, at the time of its building, was on a small, restricted budget. The budget agreed for the work, with the contractor Charles de Bergue & Co. (the second company to receive the contract for the work, after the first withdrew before work began because of the death of one of the partners), was just over £217,000 [5] – an incredibly low figure for such a massive and sophisticated undertaking. De Bergue was a known 'bridge man', having built many around the world. It was, unfortunately, a bridge too far for this already ill man, who had agreed a sum vastly under a realistic budget. He died, and the contract passed to Hopkins, Gilkes & Co., whose budget alone amounted to more than the original estimate. Unsurprisingly, the costs ran over significantly, not least because of an 'unfortunate accident' or 'storm' purported to have happened on 19 January 1887, as written in a letter by Edgar Gilkes to John Stirling (I say 'purported' as William Dow's research contradicts this date). This 'brought down two spans of the girders and partially destroyed the piers'.[6] What made this so catastrophic was, it is now believed, that the company were uninsured at the time [7] and the figures had to be renegotiated to cover some of the costs of replacements and the original bonus of £2,000, if a train was run over the bridge in September, was increased to £4,000. This was small fry when it came to the final sum. The minutes of the Tay Bridge Committee, on 28 June 1877, make reference to this:

Costs:
De Bergue & Co. – £ 93,069 2s 6d
Hopkins, Gilkes – £229,605
A total of £322,674 2s 6d
Some £63,174 in excess of estimate.[8]

What makes the £4,000 significant, is that it was not nearly the amount wanted, or needed, to cover the replacement work and, claims Dow, it is the action taken to cheaply rebuild that part of the bridge using the 'straightened girder', which (he believes) could have played a major part in the accident.

The bridge had been a long-time dream for Fifeshire residents, local business people and the railways. It was the 'blue-sky thinking' required to overcome all the difficulties; necessary changes of transport and lengthy time of travel it took to cross the Firth of Tay

(Scotland's longest river (120 miles/192km)) and travel from the capital, Edinburgh, to Dundee. Thomas Bouch, an established railway engineer, was well-known for railway construction and for designing viaducts, especially the Belah Viaduct. He was also known for doing jobs 'on the cheap', had proffered the idea of the railway bridge way back in 1854[9] and had promoted it for many years. Eventually, it was decided that a railway connection across the Tay was not just needed but was now necessary in the new fast-paced world. It would also make the NBR the largest and most viable railway company in Scotland. The North British Railway (Tay Bridge) Act eventually received the Royal Assent on 15 July 1870, and the foundation stone was laid on 22 July 1871. Because of their financial constraints, the NBR made the fateful decision to have a single track rail bridge, linking Edinburgh in the south and Dundee in the north. This brought forth many protests, even from those in favour of the bridge. One of its most vocal advocates, the *Dundee Advertiser* was so disbelieving that its proprietor personally wrote against it:

> In advocating a bridge across the Tay, it never occurred to us that any engineer would think of running such a spider's thread over the river as this is to be … what will be the use of attempting to carry the great East Coast route for more than two miles suspended between the sky and water on about the width of a respectable dining table? It assumes immense faith in railway passengers to imagine that they will trust themselves on this tight rope.[10]

However, trust they did, and the line proved to be extremely commercially successful during the short time that it ran, in both passenger and freight carriage, whilst the trust proved to be extremely ill-founded.

Those of a superstitious nature could point to the fact that there was a taste of things to come from the very beginning. Grothe, so intimately involved in the ongoing work, writes:

> The very first foundation, floated out on August 27th 1875, was severely tested by the weather. When it left the shore in tow of two steamers a gentle breeze was blowing, but by the time it reached the

place where it had to form part of the bridge the breeze had increased to a strong gale, and the waves washed over the barges so that the hatchways had to be caulked to prevent filling and sinking. It was left in that position nearly three days till the gale moderated sufficiently to allow the operation to proceed.

Eighteen months later, the bridge was once again tested by nature's forces and Grothe commented:

> Since 1871 the storm had not raged with such fierceness as on the night of February 3rd, 1877. Without any barometrical warning, it came down at four o'clock in the afternoon with an unparalleled suddenness.[11]

These incidences should have been useful portents as to the fickleness, scale and power of nature's force in this area and of nature's uncontrollable involvement in this enterprise, but sadly, they were not.

The Event

Sunday 28 December 1879 had started reasonably well weather wise. It was reasonable enough not to excite comment over the late afternoon and early evening; however, it began to get windier and, by the time the train previous to the fateful one travelled over the bridge, the wind effect was noticeable and raising comment: 'The rapid fall of the barometer indicated mischief brewing in the Tay.'[12] By the time the 4.15 p.m. train from Edinburgh arrived, a full scale storm was raging with strong gusty squalls. The storm was not confined to the Firth of Tay, it also blew across the land. In Glasgow 'the wind blew a perfect hurricane'; in Edinburgh it was strong enough to 'throw persons off their feet'; in the suburbs near the fated bridge the houses felt the 'full fury' of the wind, which blew off chimney pots, whirled slates in the air and even downed trees. The *Annual Register* wrote, on the day following the accident that the wind was '... more violent than had ever been known in the century ... a terrible hurricane struck the bridge.'

Several of the witnesses called before the Court of Inquiry also remarked on the severity of the wind. One was Captain Scott of the ex-Royal Navy Frigate *Mars,* a training ship for young boys in need of care, discipline and education, which was permanently moored in the River Tay just under a mile away from the bridge. Captain Scott knew about the quality of storms, being a seasoned seaman. Using the Beaufort Scale (originally introduced for the Royal Navy for measuring the 'force' of the winds i.e. 1–12 with 12 being the most violent), he declared that overall he considered it was a 10 (a storm), but in the gusts it measured around 10/11 (a violent storm). Several other witnesses hazarded a guess or estimate of the wind force, most agreeing that it was 'very strong'. Yet it was remarked in various journals, such as the *Saturday Review* (1880), that, despite the severity of the storm, no other bridges had fallen and the question was asked – why not?

Before official permission was given to open the bridge, Major General Hutchinson, Inspector for the Board of Trade, had tested the bridge over three days as severely as was thought necessary. He had tested it with one, two and then more engines going together across the bridge. Finally, he had had six locomotives, each weighing seventy-three tons, coupled together, go across the bridge at a speed of 40mph to test the resistance to vertical strain. He had also watched, from a boat, a train crossing the bridge. He had instructed that no train should travel at a speed higher than 25mph, and also recorded his wish to have an opportunity of observing the effects of high wind when a train of carriages was crossing the bridge. Unfortunately, this never happened.

On completion of the work it was recorded that, 'No part of the structure has shown a sign of failure although the storms, since the highest and most exposed parts of the structure were built, have been of unsurpassed severity.' It begs the question, then – was Sunday's storm the 'most violent ever known to Dundee' and if so, why was the devastation not more widespread? Writing one year later, in the *Journal of the Scottish Meteorological Society,* A. Buchan remarked that the storm had 'presented peculiarities that, taken together, made it one of the most remarkable storms yet observed in the British Isles'.[13]

The Train

'The train from Edinburgh which fell with the bridge'[14] was the regular 4.15 p.m. Sunday afternoon passenger train, carrying mails (this service was commonly known by locals as 'the Edinburgh'). The passengers began their journey at Waverley Station, Edinburgh, and travelled by local train to Granton Harbour on the south coast of the River Forth, there the passengers transferred to the ferry boat to cross the river to Burntisland, where the connecting train to Fife was waiting for them. It stopped at nearly all the wayside stations from Burntisland to Dundee. (The North British Railway had not yielded to the sabbatarian opposition in the way one of its constituent companies – the Edinburgh & Glasgow – had, and by 1879 such opposition was very much less of an issue generally.)[15]

The train from Edinburgh arrived, in due course, at St Fort Station, the final station before the bridge, at around 7.05 p.m., it was late and the tickets of the passengers for Dundee were collected as usual. William Friend, ticket collector, collected those in the third class, by the engine, and Alexander Inglis, porter at St Fort, collected those in the second class. There were no passengers in First, he stated.[16] Because of the weather conditions, Robert Morris, the stationmaster, also gave a helping hand.[17] Morris believed he was the last person to talk to the people on the train.

The ticket collectors would later inform the Inquiry that there were, on the train at that time, fifty-seven passengers for Dundee, five or six for Broughty Ferry, five for Newport (and two season ticket holders), plus the usual crew, the engine driver, stoker, and mail guard with two other guards travelling as passengers, making a total of seventy-four or seventy-five persons. (Recent research has shown that only two can be accounted for going to Broughty Ferry, and that actually, the train did not go anywhere near Newport. St Fort was the last stop in Fife.)[18]

At approximately 7.13 p.m., the engine reached Wormit signal box, the train slowed and Thomas Barclay, signalman on duty, handed the baton to the stoker, John Marshall. This was the driver's authority to proceed across the bridge knowing that no other train was there.

Barclay was the last person to have contact with the train. The train moved off at the regulatory 3mph into the darkness, and into the history books. What happened next has become the biggest mystery in the history of Fife and British railways.

Many eyes watched the train as it set off to cross the bridge.[19] The nearest were those of John Watt, who had worked with the NBR for twelve years who was also a friend of signalman, John Barclay. Watt, the older man, had gone to keep Barclay company in the Wormit signal box. Whilst Barclay, having given the baton to the fireman and struggled against the wind back into the box, was signalling, to the northern cabin, of the train's imminent arrival and noting its departure in his book, Watt's eyes were glued to the tail lamps at the back of the train. The train travelled some 200 yards before throwing out sparks from its wheels, 'after they had continued for about three minutes there was a sudden bright flash of light, and in an instant there was total darkness.'[20] Watt told Barclay what he had seen. 'Her tail lamps have gone,' he said.

Barclay was not unduly concerned, believing that the train would reappear at any minute. The bridge was not, after all, a straight one, nor a completely flat one. 'From the south shore it curved left for three spans, bringing itself at right angles to the course of the river … then it turned to the right again. It fell slightly for the first three spans, ran level for another three, then climbed an incline, of 1 in 490, to Pier 29. From here, it was level until Pier 36 where it began to fall, initially 1 in 130, but at Pier 37 around 1 in 74, until the north shore was reached. Going up and down it had the appearance of a "giant centipede treading the water".'[21]

Having finished his chores, Barclay tried to ring the signalman at the northern end of the bridge, just to check, but got no answer. He tried both the telephone and telegraph and found that they were not working. The men realised something was seriously wrong – but what? They went outside and tried to get along the bridge, but were driven back by the strength of the wind. They retraced their steps and went along the Tayport line by the shore side hoping to get a better view.

What they saw as the moon came out from behind the clouds was beyond belief – a large section of the bridge was down. The men still did not know if the train had reached the other side. Barclay needed to go back to his post in the signal box (another train was due and needed warning), whilst Watt made his way to Tayport where he informed the Company Agent what he had seen.

On the northern side of the water there was just as much consternation when the train did not arrive, and no information had been received from the southern signal box. Henry Somerville was an experienced signalman, used to discrepancies in timing, so he gave the train nine, rather than the usual five, minutes to arrive before worrying. When it still had not, he became anxious. He went to his highest view point, inside his cabin, and looked out. He could see nothing – no lights, no train. He raised the official alarm that the train had not appeared.

James Smith, Tay Bridge stationmaster (where crowds were already gathering because news, from those who had watched the train fall, had spread), and James Roberts, the locomotive foreman, who had come to the sidings to deal with wagons blown about by the force of the storm, were faced with a dilemma. How could they find out if there something was wrong with the bridge? There was only one way, unable to stand against the might of the wind, and hanging on for dear life, they crawled on hands and knees along the bridge. Smith had to stop. He could not go further, but Roberts, belly against the planks, slowly dragged and pushed himself along in the seemingly never-ending darkness, until he came to the gap in the structure. There could now be no doubt.

A telegram was sent from the stationmaster at Dundee to the NBR's Company Engineer at Portobello, near Edinburgh:

Terrible accident on Bridge – one or more of high girders blown down – am not sure as to the safety of last train down from Edinr [Edinburgh] will advise further as soon as can be obtained.

Unfortunately, when the information was released to the public, the company's statement said that there been 'about 300 passengers'. The next day the dreadful news was flashed around the world:

No. 2119.—VOL. LXXVI. SATURDAY, JANUARY 10, 1880. WITH TWO SUPPLEMENTS SIXPENCE. By Post, 6½d.

THE TAY BRIDGE DISASTER: VIEW OF THE BROKEN BRIDGE FROM THE NORTH END.—SEE PAGE 27.

The long, tortuous crawl of James Robert, locomotive foreman, out along the bridge until he reached the last pier standing. Clinging on for his life, and looking out from the north side, the scene depicted would have brought home to him the horror and enormity of the situation.

TERRIBLE DISASTER IN SCOTLAND
PART OF THE TAY BRIDGE BLOWN DOWN
LOSS OF 300 LIVES. [22]

All around the world people, like those in Dundee and Fifeshire, were stunned.

When the train from Edinburgh went into the water, it went in complete. No part was left behind. One moment it was all there, the next, with a 'flash of light', 'a flare of flames', 'a spray of sparks' (all descriptions of what eyewitnesses reported they had seen) it was totally gone. It had vanished. To paraphrase the famous words of Queen Elizabeth I after a great storm had dispersed the Spanish Armada, 'God breathed, and it was gone.' (And so said many sabbatarians, whose voices once more were raised in condemnation of such commercial activities on the Sabbath. The *Christian Herald* called it 'a judgement of the Almighty upon those who ... commit the outrage of violating the sanctity of the Lord's Day'. [23])

A whole train gone was as incomprehensible as the Tay Bridge falling down. 'At Dundee business is at a standstill. Nothing but the disaster is spoken of. The lower part of the town has been crowded all day with persons eager for information and tonight the crowd is still dense.' [24]

'The train from Edinburgh which fell with the bridge' was drawn by the No. 224, a 4-4-0 passenger engine by Thomas Wheatley which, according to Dr Euan Cameron was, when introduced in 1871, a significant engine type of its time. He writes:

Thomas Wheatley's first two 4-4-0 passenger engines were some of the most interesting and, in their own way, significant passenger locomotives to appear in the mid-nineteenth century. 224 and 264 represent the turning-point between the mid-Victorian 2-4-0 and the late Victorian era bogie passenger locomotive. They were the first inside-cylinder 4-4-0 tender locomotives with Adams bogies to run in Great Britain, and were derived very closely from a corresponding 2-4-0 class, Wheatley's two large-wheeled 2-4-0s Nos. 141 and 164. [25]

> The driving wheels were 6 feet 6 inches in diameter, and coupled;
> the cylinders were 17 inches in diameter, with a stroke of 24 inches.[26]

Ironically, this was not the 224's usual run, but it was rostered in place of a Drummond 0-4-2T, No. 89 *Ladybank*, which was having its boiler washed out.[27]

The search for the train began within minutes, but it would take days to find and weeks to retrieve it. Although the engine and its tender was located, by diver Edward Simpson, on Wednesday 31 December it remained where it was, within the girder lying on its side in the murky waters, for some considerable time. In early April 1880, concerted efforts were made to retrieve it. The first time, the chains broke. The second time, just two days later, was even more tantalising because the locomotive was raised to the surface when the salvage equipment gave way. Not until 10 April was it pulled from the waters and found to be in surprisingly reasonable condition. It stood waiting on the beach until it was sent to NBR's Locomotive, Carriage and Wagon Works at Cowlairs for repairs, and it went on its own wheels!

Once it arrived at Cowlairs and was examined properly, by Dugald Drummond, the NBR's locomotive superintendent, it was found that the throttle valve, or regulator, was fully open. The reversing lever was in the third position from mid gear and its Westinghouse brakes were not applied. One can assume, therefore, that the driver had no warning or inclination of the forthcoming disaster. If the driver had thought that anything untoward was happening, or going to happen, he would have shut down the regulator; drivers do this so often that they do it instinctively.

The engine was restored to full working order, more or less in original condition.[28] After its rescue and 'face-lift', the 224 gained a certain notoriety and, after its several 'dives', was wryly named 'the Diver' by the NBR staff. Once repaired and refurbished, it carried on working for the North British Railway until 1908. Drivers, however, refused to take another 224 across the new Tay Bridge. This was not done again until 28 December 1908, the 29th anniversary of the accident. The Secretary of the NBR, writing in a letter

dated 18 January 1911, stated: 'The engine in question is No. 224
and is employed on the Passenger service between Dunfermline and
Glasgow and Thornton. It is a bogie engine with 17in by 24in cylinders, four coupled wheels 6ft 6in diameter, and bogie wheels 3ft 7in
diameter. The engine was reboiled in 1887 and has since been in
continuous service.'

'The Diver' gained notoriety, and the carriages it pulled behind
became part of one of the several small mysteries in the whole story
(others being the real number of those who died and the numbers of
tickets collected in respect of the numbers of passengers identified.)
The carriages behind were – three third class (nos 579, 629, 650), one
first class (no. 414) and one second (no. 138), plus the guard's brake
van (no. 146).

When asked about the line-up of the train just after the
accident, Robert Morris, stationmaster at St Fort Station, stated
that there were two third-class carriages behind the engine, one
first, then another third, followed by a second and the brake
van. Dugald Drummond, as well as being the NBR's locomotive
superintendent, was a respected locomotive designer and builder.
He was a man of strong views, known for his outbursts and for
being forthright in his opinion. In his first report to the Inquiry he
confirmed this line-up. Some newspapers report this arrangement
too, 'the composition of the ill-fated train is believed to be as
follows – Engine, two third-class carriages, first-class carriage,
third-class carriage, second-class carriage, and the van.'[29] Henry
Law (civil engineer ordered by the Court of Inquiry to carry
out a full examination of the bridge and the facts) also believed
this to be so; however, intriguingly, by the time this was put into
print for the 'official statement' of the Inquiry, the positions had
changed. Allan Rodgers writes in his article in the NBRSG Special
Edition Journal, that the line-up as per the 'corrected' version was,
'a 4-wheeler Third, 6-wheeler First, 4-wheeler Third, 4-wheeler
Third, 4-wheeler Second, and a 4-wheeler brake van.' What caused
this confusion, and what really was the 'correct' version? Rodgers
argues that the original version, given by Drummond is the correct
version, based on the findings and reports of the divers. (His

adaption of an illustrative diagram, showing where they say they found the carriages and engine, appears to strongly support this.[30])

Why should we worry regarding the position of the carriages at all? Well, the type and nature (size, weight, materials) and position of the carriage may add to, clarify or defend the theories already being purported. There was, at the time of the accident, a great deal of suggestion, and argument, that the small, light nature of the second-class carriage (it weighed just 5 tons and 19cwts) would have left it vulnerable to lifting in the wind. The other carriages weighed a good deal more; the third class in front of it weighed 9 tons 16cwts and the brake van behind 8 tons 9 cwt unloaded,[31] although that night it was carrying a large number of mail bags and some luggage.

Henry Law looked seriously at the nature and position of the second-class carriage because of the proposition that this, along with the guard's van, 'tilted against the leeward girder' by the wind could have caused enough damage 'to destroy portions of the girders and occasion the fall'. This was, indeed, claimed to be the case by Sir Thomas Bouch, designer of the bridge. Mr Rothery (Chairman of the Court of Inquiry), however, questioned how such 'a very light carriage … so lightly constructed [could have] done so much injury to the bridge as to have caused more than 1,000 yards of it to fall?'[32] The debate remains very much unresolved, and continues even today.

Another reason for knowing the accurate position of the carriages was to ascertain where the highest concentration of people were. The majority of the passengers were third class, there were only eight passengers in second class and none reported in first.[33] This knowledge would have been helpful for the trawling boats and divers in their search. Would the bodies be concentrated immediately behind the engine in two carriages, or in the middle or back of the train? They would not necessarily find bodies within those carriages, but such knowledge may have helped them to begin their search where the highest concentration was thought to be. This is mostly likely what happened because the searchers would probably have been acting on the information given by 'the man on the ground' i.e. the stationmaster, rather than the later 'official' version.

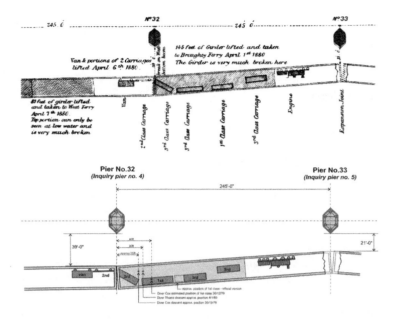

The top diagram shows the remains of the train laying within the span between pier Nos 4 and 5 of the bridge, giving the 'official' version of train layout, as stated by Dugald Drummond, the North British Railway's locomotive superintendent. Allan Rodgers of the North British Railway Study Group argues that the 'original' version is the correct version (shown in plan), as reported by diver Cox and others. (Latter courtesy of Allan Rodgers)

The first carriage to be found was the first-class carriage which was still standing upright, as were the other carriages to the front of the train. The last part of the train, the substantial third-class carriage, was finally found on Monday 26 January 1880, by Diver Fox when he descended from the barge exactly opposite the 4th pier. This carriage was lying on its side with the ends pointing to east and west and all the doors still shut. Much of the window glass was smashed and the carriage roof was off. To determine what class of carriage it was, Fox had attached a rope to one of the doors and, with the aid of the crane, it was pulled off and up. The door appeared quite new. This was the heavy rear third class and it, along with the remains of the shattered second-class carriage and guard's van, were eventually raised on Tuesday 6 April. The three vehicles had become separated from the rest of the train. Now all the carriages had been raised.

The People

Debris began arriving on the beach just a short time after the accident. The first things to wash ashore were the mail bags, some half a dozen, addressed 'From London to Dundee'. Immediately below Broughty Ferry Castle they found: a letter rack for keeping the letters in the guard's van; a tool box, presumed to be the driver's; the front part of a carriage with 'second' written upon it; and several window frames. Along with these were several items of personal clothing.

As the search went on, the items recovered from the waters and the shores were gathered in the parcels office at Tay Bridge Station to await identification. The everyday nature of the items bring home the human side of the situation, reminding us that these belonged to real people who had walked the earth just a short time before:

A lady's handbag, containing a Bible (without a name), a pair of spectacles in a case, a purse and a bunch of keys, all later identified as belonging to Anne Cruickshanks.

The guard's basket, containing two neatly rolled hand signals.

The cap of David Johnston, the guard, and the caps of the engine driver, David Mitchell, and John Marshall, the fireman.

A vest and a dress shirt rolled in a handkerchief.

A red tablecloth, two chemises and a pair of stockings tied in a handkerchief.

A packet of about 2lb of tea.

A girl's muff.

An empty hamper from Leicester for Montrose – an invoice in the hamper showed that it had contained thirty Leicester pies.

A man's felt hat.

A pair of spectacles in a case.

Two chemises and a pair of stockings tied in a handkerchief.

A gold watch was found in a box in one of the mailbags which had been washed ashore at Broughty Ferry. It belonged to Captain Thomas Nicoll of Dundee, and had been presented to him for his gallant acts for a shipwrecked crew of the American schooner *Bennington*. The watch had suffered a great deal from the salt water. Mr George Jack, secretary of the Local Marine Board, informed the Board of Trade, who replied that he should have the watch mended at their expense, which was done.

Seeing such personal, familiar items on display must have been disturbing, and incredibly distressing for the families and friends looking on with dread and even hopeless hope for news of their loved ones. The items were all placed under the charge of customs officers.

A 'search and rescue' operation was immediately set up by the Harbour Master, Captain William Robertson, whereupon he brought in boats – local fishing and whaling boats – and hired divers to go out to look for the bodies, the train and the bridge. Initially there were just three divers involved. Two were employed by the Dundee Harbour Trustees – John Cocks (he was the first diver to go down), and Peter Harley a local man who lived in Tayport, a very experienced diver – and the third was Edward Simpson, employed by the NBR. (Harley and Simpson had previously been used, in August 1873, to rescue and recover workers' bodies from down a shaft after an explosion at Pier 54. Six men had died.) There were soon more. Another diver, William Norley, a diver on board the gunboat HMS *Lord Warden* (the coastguard ship of the Firth of Forth), was sent down by his commander Captain Brine. Others were John Gray of Dundee, previously a naval reserve; John Barclay, who came up from North Shields looking for work, taken on by the NB, and Henry Watts, of Sunderland.

Henry (Harry) Watts (53) had spent all his life on the water or diving. He was something of a hero and well-known in Sunderland for good deeds, as well as his diving prowess. Over his lifetime he saved thirty-six lives. It is said that he 'did good without any thought of personal return', but he received many medals and honours in recognition of his bravery. Henry first used the diving bell in 1864. During his diving life he had many bad experiences and near-death escapes.

This dark and gloomy image shows divers in their cumbersome gear set up for 'search and rescue' operations. Whilst the people were the first priority, recovery of the bridge and the train was of vital importance in order to ascertain what had happened – and prevent its reoccurrence. Trawlermen and fishermen and their boats were hired in to help with the rescue.

One of the worst of his tasks as a diver, he said, was the recovery of dead bodies, a task which he always willingly undertook but would accept no fee or reward. At the time of the disaster, Watts was working for the River Wear Commissioners. Mr C.H. Dodds, the General Manager of the River Wear Commissioners in Sunderland, heard the news and went to his Chairman, Sir James Laing, and suggested they ask Henry Watts to go to Dundee to help. Watts agreed, offering his services for free.

The diving operations were frustrating and hazardous. Unlike the relative freedom of movement that we have today, divers of those times were greatly constrained by their equipment, which was heavy and cumbersome. They wore breast plates and lead weights on their chests and back, each weighing 28lb. In addition to this, they carried 14lb in weight on the bottom of their boots. They also had to protect the seal between their heavy airtight helmets and their suits, and to be careful of the material of their suits – Divers Gray and Watts experienced problems with ripping, and their suits filled up with freezing cold water, which was extremely dangerous for them. Needless to say they had limited vision and mobility. They, and the people on the boats watching out for them, had also to be aware, at all times, to protect their air pipes and communication lines because their lives depended on it. On top of all this, they worked in hazardous conditions, moving amongst the tumbled, dismantled columns, the broken jagged parts of the bridge, ragged iron and all sorts of debris from the train. It was also horrendously cold in and out of the water and they would have had to contend with the strong ebb and flow of the tide. Because the waters were thickly murky, especially at low tide, the divers talked of having to 'grope' and 'feel' their way.

Harry Watts did not have a good start. 'Pushing his way in the liquid darkness he stumbled upon the telegraph wires which had come down with the bridge, and in a moment he was entangled in them.' Luckily he had a new sharp knife (a must for every diver) and was able to cut himself free. He remembered the whole thing vividly – the complete darkness, 'the monster remnants of the wrecked train and bridge that could topple on top of him at any moment and crush him to death':

> The water was sometimes running like a mill race, and was so full of mud and scour that it was impossible to see anything when a few feet below the surface … [we worked] entirely by the sense of touch.
>
> … I sent up a few things and then I got into a third class carriage to look for some of the bodies, and I went through it from end to end on my hands and knees, but it was empty. In doing this a piece of iron on the carriage tore open the sleeve of my dress, which got half full of water before I could get up to put it right.
>
> … it was dreadfully heavy work, and disappointing too, owing to the state of the river and the difficulties of working amongst the huge heaps of stuff that lay at the bottom of the river. One day I came upon the engine of the train, but I dare not go in to search it, there were so many things to get entangled with.[34]

The divers had more luck with finding the train and the bridge than they did with finding the bodies. Of the first twenty two bodies, all but the first were recovered by grappling. By the end of work on

Thursday 8 January, a total of eighteen bodies had been recovered,
and by Saturday 31 January, thirty-two bodies were retrieved.

The Children

Looking at the various lists of the dead, some things immediately
leap out at one. There are nine children (under the legal age of adult-
hood at that time, which was twenty-one years).

The youngest is little Bella Neish, who was just four years, nine
months. She was travelling with her father, David (36), a teacher and
registrar, of Lochee, dressed in her pill-box hat and high buttoned
boots. The trip to visit a relative was much against her mother's
wishes, it was reported in the paper, but David so wanted the company of his 'favourite daughter' that he managed to persuade the
mother to let her go. Bella, the thirty-second body to be recovered,
was found on the beach at Wormit on Tuesday 27 January (hers was
the only body recovered upstream of the bridge). This was almost
three weeks after the recovery of her father (who was recovered on
7 January by the *Mars*), and her funeral took place just two days later.
She was interred at Balgay Hill Cemetery, and left behind not just
a grieving mother, but several siblings too. Her mother claimed the
one penny brooch Bella had been wearing.[35]

Then there are the brothers, Robert (6) and David (8) Livie
Watson, who were travelling with their father, Robert Watson, a
moulder, and were returning from a visit to friends. Mr Watson was
one of five brothers, one of whom was blind. Watson was known for
his support of the Dundee Blind Institute, and in his pocket was a
programme of a concert recently given by the charity.[36] It is reported
that his poor wife, who had been against the visit, wishing to post-
pone it until the New Year, was so overcome with grief and shock
that she had 'lost her reason and had to be admitted to the asylum'.
Father and sons were all interred at the Eastern Necropolis, Dundee.

David McDonald (10), who is identified as a 'schoolboy', was also
travelling with his father, William (41), a saw miller. Dressed in his
'Sunday best', he wore a check wincey shirt, brown ribbed stockings and a mourning cap (there had been a death in the family).[37]
Somehow, it is comforting that he was found, by the ship *Mars*, in the

same vicinity as his father, but he was not recovered until two days after, on 9 January.

All the other children are identified as being 'in jobs'.

Elizabeth Brown, just thirteen, is described as being a 'tobacco spinner'. (The 'big cigar' was a popular smoke during Victorian times and spinning and rolling the tobacco was mostly women's work.) There were four manufacturers of tobacco in Dundee at that time, and 'Lizzie', as she was sometimes called, worked at Fairweather's of Murraygate. She is amongst those who have never been recovered, along with her grandmother, Mrs Elizabeth Mann (62).

James Peebles (15) was an 'apprentice grocer' with Mr Harris of Newport. His badly decomposed body was discovered very early on Sunday 11 April (over three months after the event), by Hugh Johnstone, a mussel dredger. [38] An NBR steamer was sent to collect the body and bring it to the Dundee Mortuary, where it was formally identified. A purse with 2s 6d and a verge watch without its case were found in the pockets. The watch had stopped at 7.17p.m. [39] (Some sources state 7.16 p.m.)

Margaret Kinnear (17) was, as were many young girls and women at that time, 'in service'. A domestic servant, who had used her day off to visit her parents in Balmullo, Fifeshire, and was returning to Dundee. When she was recovered, by Captain Menzies of the Abertay Lightship, [40] she was thought, and reported by the papers, to be 'Mrs Nicoll, wife of a baker, body number 44', but she was later correctly identified by her employer, Mr Robert Lee of 6 Shore Terrace, Dundee.

The last boys, both eighteen, and both Williams, are William Threlfell, a confectioner, and William Veitch, described as 'cabinet-maker'. It is highly unlikely that Veitch was actually a cabinetmaker at such a young age. It was a skilled trade and would have required an apprenticeship which would not have finished until he was twenty-one years old. He is much more likely to have been an apprentice to the trade. Veitch's body, along with two others, was retrieved on Tuesday 13 January, and interred on the Thursday at the Eastern Necropolis, Dundee. The Eastern Necropolis was (is) an interdenominational council cemetery. Anybody being conveyed there by train probably travelled in the NBR's own 'hearse carriage', some-times irreverently called 'corpse carriage', attached to the end of a regular train.

William Threlfell's body was found almost abreast of the *Mars* ship. He had been to Edinburgh see his brother, a private in the Enniskillen Dragoons. William, known to be a devout boy, had in his pocket a book of Scriptures as well as several Christmas cards, presumably from his brother to family and friends. He also must have been part way through an apprenticeship to be a 'confectioner,' or sweet maker. (Unlike today when sweets are mass produced, the nineteenth cen-tury was a time for handmade confection. With the lowering of the price of sugar at that time, many 'sweets' as we know them today, particularly the boiled sweet type, became popular. With the growth of the new 'middle-classes' who had more disposable income, the demand for sweets increased. It would have been a fascinating job, allowing for creativity, experimentation and precision, and the sat-isfaction of having produced something that gave delight.) Threlfell was identified by his grief stricken mother. The poor woman, a widow, would have been wondering what would become of her since William, she told those around her, was her only support.[41]

Those in their Twenties

Another noticeable element from the lists is just how many of the travellers were in their twenties – twenty-nine in all, half of the known victims. Why were this group so mobile on a Sunday evening?

This was the era of industrial expansion and migration from the land and villages to the towns and cities in hope of a better life and a regular income. Most of these would have left the family home to gain better employment. Sunday was the workers' day off, and it would appear from numerous newspaper reports, that most of the young victims were on, or had been on, visits to family or friends. Travelling to see their parents had many uses. At this time there were no social services for the elderly, widowed mothers or needy siblings, so a top-up for their parents' and grandparents' income would have been welcome. It also served for family meetings, to enjoy home cooking, to get a change of clothing, and all the other things that modern day youths still do.[42] What is also noticeable, looking at this group, is that they are mostly single and only five of them are women.

David Watson (22), a commission merchant, (or assurance – what we now call an *in*surance – agent) was a partner in the firm of Wood and Watson, Baltic Street, Dundee. He is reported to have been on a visit to friends in Edinburgh. His body was retrieved a quarter of a mile east of the third broken pier. He was described as 'a youth of great promise'. He left behind a widowed mother and a heartbroken fiancée.

Thomas Annan (20), was an iron turner who worked in Wallace Works, Dundee. He was another who had been on a visit to his parents. His body was discovered on Sunday morning 11 April 1880, trapped in salmon nets at Kinshaldy Fishings, Tentsmuir, by David Stewart, a salmon fisher. This information was relayed to Constable Smith at Leuchars, who collected the body and took it back to the Old Station, placing it in one of the waiting rooms. The constable then travelled to Dundee, taking with him possessions found in the pockets and on the body, in particular an old Perth halfpenny, as well as small pieces of clothing. These confirmed that it was Annan. Confirmation was also given by his uncle and Mrs Nicholson, with whom he resided at 48 Princes Street, Dundee. He had joined the train at Ladybank, having travelled from Newburgh where his parents lived. Annan was one of several who had strong connections with north-east Fife.

Two other young men travelling together were long-time friends, Robert Fowlis (20), and fellow mason David Cunningham (17). They were employed at the 'New Lunatic Asylum' at West Green, near Lochee. They had gone on their usual Saturday visit to see family and friends in Fifeshire, where both had been born, returning on the Sunday and boarding the train at St. Fort. They trained together, worked together, lodged together, travelled together, died in this tragic accident together, lay in the mortuary together and both are buried in the churchyard at Kilmany.

Others travelling together were Archibald Bain (26), son of a farmer, from Mains of Balgay and his sister Jessie (23) who had been on a visit to their uncle in Cupar. They travelled in a second-class compartment. Archibald was recovered on 8 January, along with

Thomas Davidson (29), another farm servant of Linlathen. Archibald was rescued by whale boat No. 2 and it is reported that 'an expression of pain rested on his features.' His skull was badly fractured. Their uncle had wanted them to stay another night, but Archibald wanted to be back home to help his aged father on the farm on the Monday morning.[43] Jessie was trapped among the girders and not found by a diver until much later, on 18 February. It was reported under the heading, 'One of the more heart-touching relics from the wreckage' that there was a letter written by Jessie to her father. It was picked up by the chief boatman of the coastguard service on 8 January at Arbroath, where it has been cast ashore. It said, 'My dear father, I intend coming home on Sunday night with the 7.30 p.m. train. Hoping that you are all well and merry, kind love to all. Yours truly JESSIE BAIN, DUNDEE'.[44] Obviously Jessie had not gotten around to posting this letter. One wonders what the letter had been written with – ink or lead pencil – and how it had survived being in the water.

Yet another pair were George Johnston (24), and his fiancée, Eliza Smart (24). She had wanted to return by boat but, because of the roughness of the water, took the train instead. Like her aunt, Anne Cruickshank, who also perished, Eliza was also in service. She was sometimes identified as a 'domestic servant' and sometimes a 'table maid'. (In the hierarchy of servants a 'domestic' could be anything from a cleaner, to a kitchen/scullery help, or some other role 'below-stairs'. A table maid was an 'upstairs' domestic servant who laid and waited at the table, either in houses or in hotel dining rooms. The type of establishment would determine whether her work would include other duties or not.) Eliza is intriguing. On the outside she was dressed all in black – 'black corded dress, black tight pilot jacket, black bonnet and feather'; but underneath, she wore 'scarlet stays' and 'white stockings'. Her official description notes that she was 'very tall' but also that 'one of her legs is bandaged being smaller than the other'.[45] Being very tall, Eliza must have stood out in this short-sized community – heights for the men, where given, average around 5ft 8in/5ft 9in, with some being much shorter at 5ft 1in or 5ft 2in.

Brothers, Alexander (22) and William Robertson (20), both fire-men at Dundee Gas Works and both living at 100 Foundry Lane, also travelled together. Alexander was recovered on 8 January, but William's was the last body to be recovered (number forty-six). It was retrieved on 27 April 1880, some four months after the events; but it was as late as Tuesday 4 May before William was taken from the Mortuary and conveyed by rail to Abernethy, Perthshire for burial.

James Crichton (23), of Mains of Fintry, however, travelled alone, deep in grief. His story is like a Greek tragedy, with sorrow heaped on sorrow. He was a simple ploughman, as had been his father who had died suddenly whilst following his cart on 22 December. Crichton had been attending his father's funeral in Kettle, the family place. Little did he know that his own funeral would shortly follow. His death left his family in desperate straits. The plan had been that he would step into his father's shoes, and be the support for his mother and eight siblings. Their case was put before the Temporary Relief for the Bereaved Fund Committee, by Rev. Mr Gordon of Kettle, and it was agreed to send him £3 to give relief to the family.[46] It seems a meagre sum, even for those times, especially as the Fund was so full.

James Murdoch (21), engineer, was one of the three actually recovered by the divers. He was reported as being 'dug-out' from underneath the southernmost girder, on 7 February, by diver Tait. James Murdoch was the third child in a family of seven children. His elder brother was also an engineer. James had moved south and resided in London, but had returned north to enjoy the traditional festivities of the New Year with his parents and family.

Thomas Davidson (29), a ploughman of Linlathen, had been visiting friends in Fifeshire. He joined the train at Cupar. He was found on Thursday 8 January, embedded in the sand 400 yards east of the bridge.

Joseph Low[e] Anderson (20) had also been on a visit to his friends in Cupar. He had gone on the Saturday and had taken the return train at that same station. Anderson was an apprentice com-positor in the *Dundee Courier & Argus* office. It seems hugely ironical that his paper should be reporting his death, the finding of his body and its identification by his father, a bookseller from Auchtermuchty, along with the news of the other victims. His body was picked up by a Wick fishing boat at Ulbister, on the Caithness coast, late in April. He was one of the last, the forty-fifth body to be recovered but, because of serious deterioration, he was another who had to be identified by his clothing. The identification was assisted by the fact that he had three printer 'leads' in his pocket. When Joseph Anderson was removed from the mortuary in Wick to be carried to the railway station for the train journey home, as a mark of respect, all the compositors from the local newspapers formed up as a cortège and escorted him to the railway station.[47]

Several of the male victims, even those in their twenties, left behind family. John Lawson (25), plasterer, left a wife and two children. James Millar (27) left a wife and young child. In order to provide a better life for them, Millar had been working away from home in Dysart for the previous few months and returning to be with his young family each weekend. Smoking a pipe was a popular habit at this time, and many of the male victims had pipes and tobacco about their person – James had not one but two clay pipes on him.

Both James Leslie (21), employed by Mr John Fleming, wood merchant, and Robert Frederick Syme (22) of Nethergate employed in the Royal Hotel, Dundee, were of the 'new class' of worker – a clerk. This role had been little known before the Industrial Revolution, but with industrial expansion and the spectacular growth of the Flagships of Industry, particularly the railways, the role of the clerk grew in number and significance. Syme, single and an only son, had been on a week-long visit to his parents. He was well-regarded by his employer and, through his work, he was well known by travellers and residents of Dundee. Syme had a surprisingly large sum upon his person £12 2s 6d, as well as foreign coins and a silver English lever watch. He also had a travelling bag with his initials on it. James Leslie was obviously fond of reading and poetry, as he had with him a volume of Longfellow's poems. In keeping with his work, he also carried a pencil case, a small pocket book and a rule. He had less cash than Syme, just £1 3s 7½d, but a gold watch and a gold 'Albert'. (Watches at this time were kept in pockets and an 'Albert' (named after Prince

Albert) was a chain, either brass, silver or gold, which made access to the pocket watch easier. The chain was attached to the watch which went in the pocket and a T-bar on the chain was tucked into a buttonhole. The other end of the chain was often used for 'decorative' charms.) Leslie was buried in the Western Necropolis, Dundee.

Walter Ness (23) of Wellgate, was a foreman saddler with J.M. Storrar of Dundee. He was also a 'gunner' in the Dundee Artillery Volunteers. He had obviously had an eye with the gun, having won a silver cup in competition that autumn. His funeral was reported by the *Courier and Argus*, informing how it had been agreed by Major Urquhart that a party of non-commissioned officers and men of the 4th Forfarshire Artillery Volunteers would parade and accompany the remains for interment. The coffin was draped in the Union Jack with Ness' helmet and sword on top. Six pallbearers carried the coffin to the steamer for its short crossing to Tayport. From there it went by train to Kirkcaldy, where a large crowd of family and friends waited to take part in the service.

William Jack (23), a grocer of Scoonie, Fife, resided in Dundee but was originally of Dairsie. He had returned there to visit and comfort his grieving mother, and to offer what practical help he could; his sister had died just two weeks earlier. He attended church twice on the Sunday before catching the evening train at Leuchars. One can only imagine how his poor mother must have felt losing a daughter and a son in such a short space of time.

Robert Culross (26) of Tayport, described on his certificate as a 'carpenter', had actually served an apprenticeship as a boat-builder, but was recently employed by the NBR as an 'erector of advertising boards' to be put up at their stations. He was engaged to be married in the first week of February and was on his way to Dundee to invite friends to the wedding. His mother and fiancée identified his body.[48]

James Henderson (22), a single labourer residing in Dundee, was the eldest of eight children. He is known to have boarded the train at Ladybank. He was one of eleven recovered 'abreast' or nearby the *Mars*. Finally George Taylor (25), a mason from Dundee, was a single man travelling with a friend, Mrs Elizabeth Nicoll.

The Other Passengers

Women

Anne (Annie) Cruikshanks' claim to fame is that she was the first
to be recovered, at 9 a.m. the morning after the incident. Her body
was floating in the water near the beach at Newport. She was taken
to one of the waiting rooms at Tay Bridge Station which, at the
stationmaster's direction, had been turned into a temporary mortuary. Her recovery was eagerly reported. The papers noted that
'she had hair that had been black but was now very streaked with
grey'. It was generally agreed that she was 'decently dressed'. She
wore 'a black merino petticoat' and her long jacket was 'trimmed
with buttons down the back ... She had her left glove on and was
firmly clutching the other in her right hand.'[49] 'There was nothing
except an unmarked handkerchief her pocket'. Perhaps surprisingly,
what they did not agree on was her condition. Various descriptions
appeared: 'with the exception of a slight bruise on the forehead,
there was no mark of injury on the body' as opposed to 'her head is
severely lacerated and her left leg broken' and '... her face is a good
deal cut'.[50]

Anne (54), from Kingsbarns, was a spinster and worked for Lady
Baxter of Kilmarron, Edinburgh. She is described as a 'domestic servant' as well as 'maid to Lady Baxter'. As the latter, it would
make more sense that she was travelling second class with Mrs Mary
Easton, widow of the late Rev. James C. Easton, also in her fifties
and the cousin of Lady Baxter. Mrs Easton was travelling from
Edinburgh after visiting Lady Baxter, to see another cousin who
lived in Broughty Ferry, on the eastern outskirts of Dundee. Anne
Cruickshanks was detailed to accompany Mrs Easton. They should
have caught the morning train, but Lady Baxter's coachman slept in,
and they had to catch the evening train instead.[51]

Anne Cruickshanks also had the distinction of being the first of
the victims to be buried. Emotions amongst the residents on each
side of the Tay were strong and raw and so her funeral on Thursday
1 January 1880, just a few days after the incident, drew large crowds
and curiosity. She is buried at Kingsbarn, Kirkyard, in Fife.

Initially, Anne was wrongly identified as Mrs Mann, and then Mrs Euphemia Cheap[e], even though she was single and would have worn no wedding ring. Mrs Euphemia Cheap[e] (54), a mother of six, was also a domestic servant and 'very industrious' who had 'by her own exertions brought up a large family'. She had left Lochee on Sunday morning to spend the day with her mother, who resided with other relatives near St Fort. She left them to catch the last train to Dundee. On hearing the news that the body of an elderly woman had been recovered at Newport, and taking the general description given, three of her girls came to identify what they thought would be their mother. The girls were 'deeply affected' and taken into one of the waiting rooms to sit by the fire until things were ready. Unhappily for them, the body was not their mother, so the poor girls had to steel themselves to wait, until the next time, to do that dreadful duty again.[52]

Men

John Scott (30) was one of only three bodies recovered by the divers, he by the diver Harley near the fourth broken pier. His body, described as that of a young man, smart in appearance and short in stature, was found entangled in the telegraph wires in a girder and its release was a long job that took several hours. He had in his pockets a waterproof cover of a cap, two handkerchiefs and a seaman's discharge note. He had only been discharged on 24 December at Hartlepool. His father came from the poorhouse to identify his son, who, he informed the authorities, had for some time been in America. He was called the 'American sailor' by the press. His mother, separated from his father, also came to identify that body. It was profoundly sad that the young man had failed to see his parents, whom he had come back to visit after a long absence. His funeral service was conducted in the mortuary by the Rev. Mr Sugden of St Mary Magdalen's Episcopal Church. His body was conveyed to the Eastern Necropolis and interred there.

Mr Peter G. Salmond (44) was another interred in this cemetery. Mr Salmond's body had been discovered in a rather poor state, at a spot opposite Milton Railway Siding, by a young woman, a milliner named Margaret Baird, who had been walking on the beach. As the face was badly decomposed, the body had to be identified by the clothing, which was done by his son and only child, Peter. Salmond, like several others on the train, wore black since he was returning home from attending a funeral of a relative at Kirkcaldy. His own funeral was on Tuesday 14 February.

The remains of another much decomposed body was picked up 1 mile below the bridge, on the south shore of the Tay. It was discovered by Mr William Brown, a gardener, who was out walking along the beach. He saw the body of a man floating in the water and waded out to retrieve it. He informed the police at Newport, who forwarded the information on to Dundee. Mr Smith, a local undertaker, and a police official took the boat to Newport and brought the body back to the mortuary at Dundee. Although not formally identified, it was thought by the police to be that of Mr William Henry Beynon (40). Ironically, great efforts had been made to recover Beynon's body through dives. Diver Harley had gone down several times at the request of Beynon's friends. On Tuesday 13 January, Harley had made two descents between the fourth and fifth broken piers. On his return he stated that he had found the first-class carriage, which he had gone through and found nothing, and that the third-class carriage appeared to have 'driven into the first-class carriage in a telescope fashion maybe in the falling'. [53]

Beynon was described by the papers as an 'art photographer and lithographer' and 'a partner in Messrs Beynon & Co., fine art publishers and engravers, Cheltenham.'[54] He had come north on the firm's business. He was obviously a successful businessman as he had a good amount of gold jewellery about his person – a gold ring, a gold watch and Albert, gold studs and sleeve links in his shirt, and two gold appendages, one of them a spade guinea. He was also found to be a member of the Masons, as in his scarf was a Masonic gold pin.

Immediately upon receiving the news of the body being found, a close family friend, Mr Tweeney from Swansea (Beynon had been born in Wales), came to deal with the situation and make the necessary arrangements. At the mortuary he had no trouble in identifying his friend from his features, his two false teeth and all the items of jewellery upon him. According to Tweeney, Beynon had also been carrying a large amount of money, around £70 in Bank of England and Scottish notes, probably in his coat pocket, but neither were found. Mr Tweeney was given some information that may well have been distressing for him. He was told that his friend was found without an overcoat and with his vest unbuttoned. Mr Tweeney stated that his friend was 'an expert swimmer and a man of great courage and determination', and that he had no doubt whatever that he had 'begun to throw of[f] his clothing in order to swim for his life'.[55] This was, as the article then pointed out, very disturbing news, not just that Beynon's family would never know whether he had died on impact, or perished while trying to swim ashore, but that there was a very real possibility that the passengers on the train knew, even momentarily, that they were in mortal danger. (It has been calculated that there were about thirty seconds between the accident beginning and the train and bridge hitting the water.[56]) The article goes on to say that this view is supported by the expression of 'great fear' featured on one of the guards face. This possibility is further strengthened by the fact that two other male passengers were found without their coats on, as if they too had 'made ready'.

Mr Beynon's body was prepared according to the instructions conveyed to the undertakers Messrs Smith & Sons, Nethergate. It was dressed and encased in three coffins – the first a 'common black shell, which was then encased in an air-tight lead coffin and these were enclosed in a coffin of polished oak.[57] On Tuesday 10 February 1880, Beynon's coffin was sent on off on the 3.15 p.m. train for Cheltenham, accompanied by his good friend Mr Tweeney, and Mr Smith, the undertaker, who travelled with him as far as Edinburgh.[58] Beynon left a widow and two children, one aged eleven and the other aged nine.

Identifying the bodies was often problematic, especially after they had been in the water any length of time and depending on where they were discovered. Also, if they were recovered with the grappling iron they were more likely to be damaged. Sometimes there were initial mistakes, one of which occurred with the body of John Sharp (33), a joiner, who was first thought to be John Scott, the 'seaman from America'. Sharp worked for Messrs Keiller & Sons, confectioners. Unmarried, he resided in lodgings in Commercial Street, and his eventual accurate identification was made by Elizabeth Don (Rose) his landlady. Like so many others on the train, he had been returning from visiting his family – his aged parents in St Andrews. He was their sole support. Again, like several others, his body was found close to the training ship, this time by whale boat No. 10, under the charge of Robert Fairweather. [59]

George McIntosh (43), a goods guard with the Caledonian Railway, was also initially thought to be someone else. He was found a long way off from the others, some 30 miles away, cast ashore in Lunan Bay (northwards, between Arbroath and Montrose) during a violent storm, and not until 21 February. Consequently, his features were badly deteriorated which made the identification difficult. Like passenger Beynon, he was also lacking his coat. He was the thirty-sixth body to be recovered.

David Jobson (41), an ex-Councillor, of 3 Airlie Place, Dundee, was the son of a former Provost and himself a prominent local citizen. He was the thirty-seventh body to be recovered, on 17 February 1880, near Newport. Jobson was a more-than-comfortably-off oil and colour merchant (whose widow was wealthy enough to hire her own solicitor to fight the NBR, and so received by far the best compensation of all – over £5,000); however, in death, he was just the same as everyone else, an innocent victim.

William Peebles (39) was a gardener in Broughty Ferry, and had moved as a gamekeeper to Corriemony, to the west of Drumnadrochit, in the Great Glen. He needed to attend his father-in-law's funeral. He would have had to leave home on the Saturday, travel to Inverness, then down to Perth. His journey would have had to be broken somewhere overnight on Saturday, before continuing towards Dundee by way of Fife. The railway system was made up from different companies, with some of them not working on Sundays. Unfortunately, the direct rail track from Perth to Dundee was owned by one of the companies who did not work on Sundays. [60] He left a wife and eight children aged between fifteen months and fifteen years.

The NBR Staff

David Mitchell (36) of Leslie, Fife, was the driver of the train. He had worked for the NBR for sixteen years. 'He had commenced cleaning engines in early 1864, was made a fireman in 1865 and promoted to the position of driver in 1871.'[61] He was a well-regarded man and driver, and whilst working as a fireman, according to the papers, had some frightening narrow escapes but had 'saved the day' on several occasions. A married man, he left a wife and five young children aged between thirteen months and eight years. His body was not found until nine weeks after the accident. For years he lay in an unmarked grave, until Ian Nimmo-White, the secretary of The Tay Rail Bridge Disaster Memorial Trust, traced the grave and he, and the community of Mitchell's hometown, Leslie, raised funds and effected a headstone to be erected over the grave in April 2011. Mitchell's wife, Janet, and baby daughter, Margaret, also lay in unmarked graves and their names, along with his son, Thomas, and daughter, Isabella, were added to the headstone. Perhaps, in a little way, this addresses the injustice of the parsimonious assistance and compensation that this family, along with the vast majority of the other victims' families, received.[62]

John Marshall (23), stoker/fireman (both descriptions were used), was on duty. He had started cleaning in 1875 and was made up to fireman at the end of the following year.[63] When he was found his face told a sad story. His teeth were firmly clenched and his face was badly burned from falling forwards onto the firebox, or from flames rushing out and up to him as the engine plunged downwards.[64] He also had two deep wounds, one above the right eye and the other on the left cheek. He was the seventh recovery, on 7 January. He left behind a mother and two brothers.

Donald Murray (49) was the mail guard (on duty), and hailed from Inverness. He had worked for the Post Office for almost twenty years, first on the coach and then on the Edinburgh to Dundee mail route. Twice married, he left a widow with two young children, and two grown-up children from his first marriage.

David McBeth (44) was the railway guard on duty and was easily distinguishable in his railway uniform. An unmarried man, and with his father deceased, his 'worldly goods' (2s 9d, watch key, whistle, knife, comb, brass Albert, keys, India rubber and snuff box) were collected by James McBeth, his brother.[65] He was recovered on 13 January and was buried at Forfar.

Two off-duty NBR employees were travelling as passengers. David Johnson (31), a railway guard, was from Abbeyhill in Edinburgh. He was recovered by the crew of a boat under the command of David Deuchars, then District Goods Manager at Dundee, on Monday 5 January. He had been deeply embedded in the sand near the ship *Mars*. Johnson was the second person recovered, but the first in the new year of 1880.[66] He was a married man with two children. His father was a farmer, but David, like many children of agricultural workers of that time, had left the land for the railways in the hope of a better wage and a better life. When David was taken from the mortuary for burial, on 8 January 1880, his coffin was carried on the shoulders of four NBR guards, who placed it in a hearse waiting at the station; this proceeded to Craig Pier and the coffin was then taken by the eleven o'clock steamer to Newport. His body was buried that afternoon in Kemback, Fife. The other NBR employee was George Ness (21) of Tayport, newly made up stoker/fireman, who left a wife and a baby daughter just ten weeks old. It is believed he travelled on the footplate along with his friends.[67] He was recovered on 13 January, in the river near the bridge and is buried at Tayport Kirk graveyard.

How Many Victims?

The interest and concern for the case, although no longer mainstream news, continued across the country for months. On 11 March 1880, the *Portsmouth Evening News* reported that the body of George Taylor was recovered – he was number forty. He was found 2 miles east of Tayport in the River Tay. Not all the bodies were recovered. The position where the train went into the water was known for its deep, shifting, treacherous quick sands. One of the grim concerns was that, if the bodies were not recovered quickly, they would become 'embedded in the sands' and lost for all time. This may have happened to the women, in their long, heavy and cumbersome clothing. Some retrieved bodies had been swept a good way from the site, like Taylor, so others may have been swept even further. Others just eluded rescue. Jessie Bain was the second body found, but she eluded the grappling hooks and sank; she was identified by her tortoiseshell hair comb. Thursday 15 January was another frustrating and disappointing day when three bodies, two women and a man, were lost from the grappling hooks just as they were within reach. It is said they were carried off by the current. They were not the only women who had been seen by boat crews but not retrieved by them (three in one day reported by the *Glasgow Herald* on 9 January). This may have been for several reasons, not just physical – taboos, superstitions or extreme 'delicacy' may be amongst them. The recovery operation would have been greatly troublesome for these nineteenth-century mariners, who lived and breathed the ancient customs of the seas. Such customs and beliefs were deeply embedded in their bones, as much as sea water was in their blood. Women and the dead on-board a boat went against all maritime traditions, yet their 'Christian duty' and saving local people would have made them want to be helpful – that, and the money they were being paid.

The numbers given for 'not recovered' are open-ended. Due to recent research by the Tay Valley Family History Society and the 'Tay Rail Bridge Disaster Memorial Trust' it is now believed that the original seventy-five thought lost is nearer sixty or perhaps even fifty-nine. The original number, which is most commonly quoted, is based on the explanation and number arrived at in in Yolland and Barlow's joint report (section IV):

The recovery of the dead was a lengthy process and ghastly affair. Only three were found by the divers brought in to look for them. Some were 'trawled' and others were found beached. Many were in a state of deterioration and some would have been mutilated by the grappling hooks. Others 'escaped' in the rescue process – a number of which were women.

> We were told by the ticket collectors that there were at that time in the
> Train 57 passengers for Dundee, five or six for Broughty Ferry, five for
> Newport, two season ticket holders, the engine driver, stoker, and guard
> of the train and two other guards 74 or 75 persons altogether.

The Times, in its full and detailed report just two days after the accident, lists the tickets collected as:

> 2nd Class – 2 Edinburgh, 1 Glasgow Railway Officials' tickets;
> 3rd Class – 2 King's-cross, London, 1 Burntisland and 1 St Andrew's,
> 12 Edinburgh, 2 Ladybank, 1 Dysart, 7 Perth, 1 Kirkcaldy, 1 Leslie, 1
> Dairsie, 5 Newburgh, 2 Abernethy, 8 Lechars, (two are halfs), 8 Cupar,
> 1 St. Fort.= 56.

It reports that there were a number of children who may have been
travelling on their parents' tickets, and a man with several children,
one in his arms. It also states that there were about five passengers
for Broughty Ferry and a few other 'through passengers', although
their number is not known, and at least two season ticket holders. It
categorically states that the two third-class tickets from King's Cross,
London, belonged to 'two young ladies both about eighteen' – yet
the only person in the lists (of dead or missing) noted as travelling
from London is James Murdoch.[68]

   The Aberdeen Weekly Journal says that the fifty-six tickets collected at
St Fort Station comprised, 'three second –class (two from Edinburgh,
one from Glasgow), and 53 third-class', [69] and, in its 31 December
issue, it prints the 'official list' compiled by the 'station agent at
St Fort.' This identifies seventy-five travellers, whilst pointing out
that this did not take into account the children, which could bring
the number to ninety. By 13 January however, it is talking about just
sixty-two persons. Not one of them makes mention of a first-class
ticket, nor indeed does the report or the station personnel, which is
strange (as with many things to do with this mystery), since it does
not make sense that someone of William Beynon's wealth and status
would not travel first class. In addition, John Prebble, in his well-
known and respected book, *The High Girders*, gives animated detail of

a conversation said to have taken place in a first-class compartment. He also gives the name of the man who owned to having had that conversation, and to having been with Beynon in a first-class compartment – a Mr William Linskill, who was definitely travelling first class, but, upon his horse-carriage being found to take him to St Andrews, he had alighted at Leuchars. It is highly unlikely that Beynon would have then left the carriage and braved the dreadful weather to walk along to the rear end of the train, to sit in the second-class carriage. Even more unlikely is it that he entered a third-class carriage, which would have been on either side of the first class.

The *Dundee Courier*, 4 September 1935, wrote that there was a total of fifty-four tickets collected at the time, and that Robert Morris (stationmaster) had been given permission to keep them. It said that he had them mounted in a diamond shape in a frame and, when he died in 1935, the 'relic' was bequeathed to his son who had emigrated to New Zealand. This, however, is not entirely accurate as it is now believed the collage was made up in New Zealand by his descendants a long time after the event. The tickets collage has since been closely studied by The Tay Rail Bridge Disaster Memorial Trust, and they found discrepancies. For example, two return tickets issued London to Dundee, which begs the question – were this pair not going back? Also, the number of tickets does not exactly match the number of victims with the stations. In fact, one ticket has been cut in two with a razor blade, the halves separated, and made to look like two tickets. Another oddity is one ticket, from St Andrews to Dundee, supposedly issued on the Sunday when the rail link between St Andrews and Leuchars did not run on Sundays. As there are only fifty-four tickets that also begs the question – who was fare dodging? It is very possible (and probable) that, in struggling with the dreadful storm, some 'human error' occurred in the collecting of tickets, and even greater possibility of discrepancies in the forwarding of the relevant and correct number of tickets from the mass that would have been thrown in the ticket drawer, along with all the others collected that day. The evidence that the Tay Valley Family History Society cite for the number of dead being fifty-nine is the fact that this number were registered as dead in the accident, and only fifty-nine death

certificates (forty-seven males and twelve females) were issued by the
Dundee Registrar, James Anderson. As well as the fact that no other
persons were enquired of or reported missing after that, despite the
enormous coverage given by the press.

Those definitely known not to have been recovered number thirteen – five males and eight females – and include four married, or
widowed, women:

Mrs Elizabeth Mann (62)

Mrs Euphemia Cheape (54)

Mrs Mary Marion Montgomerie Easton (52)

Mrs Elizabeth Nicoll (24), of Dundee, travelling with friend George
Taylor

Elizabeth (Lizzie) Hendry Brown (13)

Eliza Smart (24)

Elizabeth Milne (21), single, dressmaker

Annie Spence (22), single, weaver

David Graham (27), single, teacher at Dalmany Sessional School

William Nelson (31), machine fitter of Gateshead

John Hamilton (34), grocer and spirit dealer of Dundee, who left a
wife and three children

Donald Murray, on-duty mail guard (49)

David Scott, goods guard (26)

These people do not have headstones – some just have a mention
on others – but now there is a memorial near by Tay Bridge to
acknowledge all victims with monuments stones with the names of
all the known dead on.[70]

The administration centre for the river was, and still is, Dundee,
with the parish being St Mary's 282/2. All of the deaths, recovered
or not, were recorded in the Register of Deaths of St Mary's Parish
in the City of Dundee, under the pen of James Anderson, registrar.
James Leslie and David Neish are entered on page 28, one under the
other, numbers 83 and 84. George McIntosh, railway guard and David
Jobson, oil merchant, are recorded on page 47, numbers 139 and 141
respectively. (They are divided by James McIntosh who died of con-

sumption.) Under 'When and where died' it states the date each was
found and at what time. Under 'Cause of death' it states for every one
of them, 'Accidentally Drowned from fall of Railway Train and portion
of Tay Bridge into River Tay on December 28, 1879', and underneath
this, for each of them is written 'Not certified'. This was/is not an
uncommon practice and usually happens if there are any questions
about the death or the cause of death, or relating to the dead person,
still to be answered. It is a matter of course if there is an inquiry. All
the recovered bodies would have undergone a post mortem (however
basic) and, as was usual, would have been investigated by a Sherriff in
court under the Fatal Accident Inquiry procedure; however, as this
was a unique incident and a much bigger inquiry was taking place, it
was the Procurator Fiscal who finally signed off on the certificates and
so all shared the same 'Cause of death' – drowning.

They then appear in the 'Register for Corrected Entries' (much
later after the closure of the Court of Inquiry). This always starts
the same way, 'The Following Report of result of a Precognition
has been received touching the Death of … (name is inserted), registered under No…. in the Register Book of Deaths for the Year
1880'. For David Neish, in his corrected entry the 'Age' differs from
the previous entry. In the book entry he is given the age of thirty-
seven years but on the 'Corrected Entry' it is given as 'thirty-six or
thirty-seven'. The ages were given by the person registering the
deaths. Sometimes, they were not all that close to the deceased, or
did not know their age, and so guessed. Some are only slightly out,
and others more than that.[71] More importantly, the wording of the
'Cause of death' has been rearranged so now it reads, 'Drowning
from fall of Tay Bridge and Passenger Train into the River'. In legal
terms this is vastly different, however, as both the train and the bridge
were the property of the North British Railway, so they were liable
for both, one wonders what was to be gained from this emphasis.[72]

Neish and Leslie are certified by both the Procurator Fiscal and
James Anderson, but not until 16 August 1880. McIntosh and Jobson
are not certified until 19 August (on page 93). The St Mary's Register
of Death was closed for the Tay bridge victims at the beginning of
September 1880.

The Inquiry

A formal Inquiry was immediately set up by Lord Sedon of the Board of Trade under the 'Regulation of Railways Act, 1871; its purpose to investigate 'the causes of and circumstances attending an accident which took place on the railway bridge crossing the Firth of Tay.'[73]

The Team
The Inquiry team had three members, each extremely experienced and knowledgeable in their own spheres, they were also the 'best man for the job'. The Board of Trade choices seem obvious – a man for each problem. Because they were dealing with a wreck at sea, they brought in the Commissioner of Wrecks, Mr Henry Cadogan Rothery, who was appointed Chairman. A mathematics graduate who trained as a barrister and practised extensively in the admiralty courts, he held many positions of senior responsibility in relation to the admiralty and, on account of this vast experience, he was appointed Wrecks Commissioner in 1876. Mr Rothery was not a man afraid to make up his own mind, even against prevailing thinking, and could be robust with his words – and so it proved. At the conclusion of the Inquiry, he felt it necessary to present his own report separately to the jointly submitted report of the other two.

Since it was a railway accident the Inquiry also had to involve the Government's Railway Department, and as this was a very serious railway accident, it was obvious to have the Chief Inspector of Railways, Colonel William Yolland. He was commissioned into the Royal Engineers in 1828, aged just sixteen, and finished his technical training at the Royal School of Military Engineering (RSME) in 1831. Appointed as an inspector of railways under the Board of Trade in July 1854, he became Chief Inspector in 1877. Influenced by his work as a railway inspector he became a zealous advocate for improved safety on the railways.

Lastly, because this was also a huge civil engineering disaster, the final member recruited was Mr William Henry Barlow, FRS, FRSE, FICE, MIMechE, a distinguished and practising civil engineer, as well as being the President of the Institute of Civil Engineers at that time. Barlow was an experimenter and inventor in his own right (he had already patented a design for a rail without the need for sleepers), and had a particular interest in the use of steel in the construction of bridges. Barlow would learn a lot from this investigation, and utilised that knowledge to his own advantage – in the designing of the second Tay Bridge.

The manner in which the Inquiry was conducted was to set a new model and protocol for any railway accident inquiries that followed – it was the CSI of its day. It interviewed eyewitnesses; took 'expert' opinion; gathered reports from organisations/companies involved and required 'material evidence'. For this they instructed an independent, but experienced, assessor, Mr Henry Law, a member of the Institution of Civil Engineers and 'expert' witness in many railway matters. Law was required to:

1. make a 'careful' inspection of the remaining structure
2. record the current situation (this included the taking of photographs)
3. take 'specimens' of the materials used (for testing in an 'independent' foundry)
4. evaluate design and construction i.e. fit for purpose
5. investigate the case of 'wind-pressure'
6. assess possible causes of accident and report back

Photographs revolutionised the examination of evidence by allowing access to 'first-hand' viewing and, thus, overcoming the obvious physical difficulties *in situ*. Photography had made great strides from its birth in the early 1800s and, with Fox Talbot's negative–positive process patented in 1841 it had gained momentum. The next big leap in development, that of the 'dry plates' had taken place just the year before the accident, in 1878, and it is probably this process that was used by the hired photographers, James Valentine & Sons. The fifty photographs were taken from four vantage points covering north, south, east and west.[74] They did not make happy viewing, showing collapsed piers, broken lugs and damaged tie bars and struts.

They were, however, an enlightening resource then, as now, for all the subsequent examination of the evidence.

The Sessions

An initial session examining local witnesses, such as those who had seen the event, was held at Dundee on Saturday 3 January 1880, and continued on the Monday and Tuesday, with Mr Trayner, chief counsel, appearing for the Board of Trade, and a Mr Balfour for the NBR. After this, it was adjourned to allow further investigation and gathering of evidence. Upon hearing that more local witnesses had been found, or come forward – those who were involved in the construction and maintenance of the bridge – sessions were resumed in Dundee between 26 February and 3 March. Then there was a waiting period. After receiving Mr Law's report dated 9 April, and the material required from the NBR, the Court of Inquiry resumed at Westminster on Monday 19 April and concluded on Saturday 8 May. The speed of the whole affair was remarkable.

When the Court of Inquiry sat to examine the evidence put before them, the questions they were seeking answers to were these:

> Did the bridge fall, causing the train to fall too? If so, why?
> Did the train derail, and take the bridge down? If so, how?
> Did the wind blow the bridge down? If so, what was the force of the wind that could achieve this?
> Was the design of the bridge at fault, making the bridge vulnerable from the very beginning? If so, in what way?

It is recorded that the Inquiry heard from 121 witnesses. In his book, *The Bridge is Down*, Andre Gren identifies 102, and why they were questioned. The breadth of witnesses is extensive – NBR officials and railwaymen (drivers, firemen, guards, station personnel, signalmen); previous passengers; contractors and construction workers; maintenance workers and painters; foremen and workers of the Wormit Foundry; inspectors; engineers; wind-pressure experts;

eyewitnesses to the fall; admirals and seamen; divers and boatmen; even a lighthouse keeper. What they had to say exposed a catalogue of woe – cavalier indifference to responsibility by those in charge (such as Bouch, or his representatives, not checking the work of sub-ordinates or the integrity of the building work); ineptitude of those in charge (NBR's bridge inspector, Henry Noble, had no idea that his repairs to the tie-bars were inherently dangerous, masking a very serious situation); irresponsible and dangerous manufacturing prac-tice (not testing the quality or reliability of the ironworks); wanton covering up of defective parts (such as the use of the 'Beaumont Egg' (a composition of beeswax, rust and other things to hand) for plugging and filling 'blow-holes' before machining); negligent and cost-cutting building (reusing damaged girders, and repairing dam-aged lugs rather than the replacement of parts); disregard of safety directives (driving the train at speeds in excess of the 25mph recom-mended). The damning information went on and on.

To examine all the evidence, engineering and otherwise, would need a book in itself. This is not the place for it. Others have done such examination in detail – David Swinfen, in *The Fall of the Tay Bridge*, provides substantial historical context and background infor-mation, and Peter Lewis, in his book, *Beautiful Railway Bridge of the Silvery Tay*, brings technical application and engineering know-how to interrogate the theories and probabilities. Others at the time, such as Henry Law, also applied engineering thinking to analyse the evi-dence as it was known to them. His report was restricted to the part of the bridge that had fallen, that part known as 'the High Girders' which towered 27ft high:

> The length of the portion of the bridge that has fallen is 3,149 feet consisting of three separate girders, the southernmost one being 1,225 feet in length, divided into five equal spans, each of 245 feet, the middle girder being 944 feet in length, divided into four spans of which the two outer ones are each 227 feet and the two inner ones each 245 feet, and the northernmost girder which is divided into for equal spans, each 245 feet. It will thus be seen that the fallen portion of the bridge con-sisted of eleven spans, each of 245 feet, and two spans each of 227 feet.

The badly damaged bridge as seen from the south bank is a sorry sight.

The 'high girders' brought low – the girders could be seen exposed at low tide. This view, looking south, shows a bridge now going nowhere.

Overall, Law succinctly concluded, 'the base of the pier was too narrow' and 'the yielding of struts and ties was the immediate cause of the disaster', this situation meant that the bridge was vulnerable to being overthrown by lateral pressure from the wind, but that 'the other circumstances stated contributed to it'.

The Conclusion

A report, dated 30 June 1880, was submitted to 'THE RIGHT HONORABLE PRESIDENT OF THE BOARD OF TRADE'. Whilst it is agreed by those who have extensively examined the transcripts of the Inquiry that every possible aspect was covered, it is also agreed that the interrogation of the witnesses and the material was not what it should have been, and opportunities for really understanding what had happened were missed. Contradictory evidence (such as the northern part of the bridge went first/the southern part of the bridge fell first) was allowed to pass without further probing; whilst officials were allowed 'wriggle-room' to evade uncomfortable questions; and controversial statements such as, 'he was mental', went without comment or challenge. At the end, the Court of Inquiry issued not one but two reports: 'REPORT OF THE COURT OF INQUIRY' and 'REPORT OF MR ROTHERY'. This is because Mr Rothery felt compelled to state and investigate certain matters more deeply and strongly than his two colleagues. The points they all generally agreed upon were:

> There is no evidence to show that there has been any movement or settlement in the foundations of the piers
>
> The wrought iron was of fair quality
>
> The cast iron was also fairly good, though sluggish on melting
>
> The girders were fairly proportioned for the work they had to do
>
> The iron columns, though sufficient to support the vertical weight of the girders and trains, were owing to the weakness of the cross-bracing and its fastenings, unfit to resist the lateral pressure of the wind

The imperfections in the work turned out at the Wormit foundry were due in great part to want of proper supervision

The supervision of the bridge after its completion was unsatisfactory

If by loosening of the tie bars the columns got out of shape, the mere introduction of packing pieces between the gibs and the cotters would not bring them back to their positions

Trains were frequently run through the high girder at much higher speeds than at the rate of 25 mph

The fall of the bridge was probably due to the giving way of the cross-bracing and its fastenings

The imperfections in the columns might also have contributed to the same result[75]

After all the hard work the report was, at best, wishy-washy with many qualifying statements using descriptions such as 'fairly good', 'probably due', 'might have', and at worst it is what we would now call a 'whitewash'. Rothery went on to address more specifically the problems raised and the theories suggested, including defects in design, making comparisons with other bridges, and asking – and answering – who was responsible? Who was to blame? Something that his counterparts were loath to do, surprisingly in Yolland's case with his reported zeal for improving railway safety. Rothery did not pull his punches, he stated:

This bridge was badly designed, badly constructed, and badly maintained … its downfall was due to inherent defects in the structure, which must sooner or later have brought it down.

For these defects both in the design, the construction, and the maintenance, Sir Thomas Bouch is in our opinion [i.e. Rothery's opinion] mainly to blame. For the faults of design he is entirely responsible. For those of construction he is principally to blame in not having exercised that supervision over the work … for the faults of maintenance he is also principally, if not entirely to blame in having neglected to maintain such an inspection over the structure, as its character imperatively demanded.

Sir Thomas Bouch, railway and bridge designer, was knighted by Queen Victoria for his work on the magnificent Tay Bridge. Whilst his name is forever linked with the bridge's disaster, he had achieved many other real engineering successes prior to that. Bouch unfairly bore the blame for what happened, which ruined his name and reputation. His memorial is a somewhat modest affair which obviously reflects his family's wish not to court attention at the time of his death, in the light of the recent happenings. It merely says 'Sir Thomas Bouch Civil Engineer, Born 29 Feb. 1822, Died 30 Oct. 1880'. Bouch's death certificate states his cause of death as, 'Disease of Heart 4 years. Chronic Pleurisy 5 months. Kidney Disease 6 months. Dropsy 21 days', but many would argue that he died of the shame and a broken spirit. (Murray and Clare Nicoll)

It was the end of Sir Thomas Bouch, his reputation and career. Now, not only would he not be permitted to continue to build the bridge across the Forth, he would not build anything again. Such a damming indictment may have hastened the man's death, just ten months and two days later, from existing illness. It was grossly unfair that this one man should bear the burden of guilt and shame that others definitely shared. In contrast, the North British Railway Company, the contractors, the Wormit Foundry, the Inspectors, even the Board of Trade's Inspector, Major General Hutchinson, all slithered across the pages with but mild admonishments.

On 1 July 1880, just six months after the accident, the *Star* reported that, 'the inquest on the Tay Bridge disaster terminated in a verdict exonerating the railway authorities from all blame'. The verdict caused almost as much shock as the accident had. The *Scotsman* was outraged, and voiced what many believed and felt:

> There was evidently a degree of carelessness in the matter of supervising the bridge which was culpable even scandalous. Sir Thomas Bouch may be to blame for not having looked after Henry Nobel; but ought not someone to have seen that Sir Thomas Bouch attended his duty? Can the railway company be freed from blame? It is very

difficult to do so ... it is clearly the company and the company alone
that must be held answerable to the public for whatever carelessness
there was in the supervision and maintenance of the bridge. [76]

The matter regarding a Public Prosecution had been raised by the
Hon. Mr Anderson MP in the House of Commons, but it had been
deferred to the Lord Advocate[77] and that was it.

John R. Raynes, in his comprehensive work, *Engines and Men:
the History of the Associated Society of Locomotive Engineers and Firemen*,
later asked, '... was the trenchant exposure of jerry-building and bad
designs of the Tay Bridge followed by prosecution, even though four-
score lives were lost? Not at all – there were words – just words – and
the matter was allowed to die out ... but poor McCulloch whose
mistake cost no life was sent to gaol.'(William McCulloch was a driver
for twenty-six years on the Caledonian Railway, all without any
mishap until the day his train collided with another when his Clarke
& Webb's patent chain brake failed to operate. He was prosecuted for
'an error of judgement' and sentenced to four months imprisonment.)

The Inquiry did, however, find that there was no requirement issued
by the Board of Trade in respect of wind pressure, and, just as significantly, that there did not appear to be any understood rule or model
in the engineering profession regarding wind pressure upon railway
structures. It recommended that the Board of Trade should take steps
for the establishment of rules for that purpose. The Board of Trade
accordingly instigated a commission to carry out the first systematic
investigation of this problem, and in May 1881 the 'Wind Structure'
(Railway Structures) Commission reported their conclusions.

The NBR were hit hard financially by the event. It is reported in
the *Dundee Courier*, on Thursday 29 January, that a circular had been
sent to the heads of department in the company, with the suggestion that 'officials and others in the employment of the Company
should subscribe to the best of their ability to a fund which it is
intended to aid the directors in the repairing of the ... bridge.' Such
was the company's financial difficulty that, once the settlements from
the Relief Fund had been made (set up with donations, to help the
families of the victims who were in dire need and with, because of

parsimony by its administrators, a hefty balance left over), the NBR asked for their donation of £500 to be returned. In respect of the claims for compensation, the NBR were Scrooge-like in holding their purse strings tightly closed. Donald Cattanach writes, in his study of G.B. Wieland, the Secretary of the NBR:

> At the Board meeting on 17th March, 1881, Wieland had reported the settlement of the whole of the personal compensation claims for just £21,632.23. Most of the sums were for a few hundred pounds, and several were settled for just double figures. Only a few exceeded £1,000. The largest settlement – for £5,436.14 – was awarded to the family of ex-Councillor David Jobson. Not a single case resulted in court proceedings although at least one summons was served on the North British Railway: the widow and family of David Johnston, a NBR guard who had been travelling as a passenger on the ill-fated train, prior to working back the following morning, were claiming £1,500. Like the few other claims which he brought to the Board's attention, it was remitted back to Wieland to deal with; they received £200.[78] The 'Widow Mitchell' – Mrs Janet Mitchell, wife of the driver of the ill-fated train, David Mitchell – received £150 for herself and her three children. Wieland took legal advice from the Solicitor General about the claim on behalf of the mother of another NBR employee, train guard David McBeth, aged 38 and unmarried. Owing to the 'adverse nature' of the Opinion, Wieland was authorised to settle the claim 'on the best terms possible.' It was settled for £250.[79]

In respect of the bridge and its future, it had not taken long for voices to be raised asking for a new bridge, such had been its success and convenience. As early as 5 January a 'Special Meeting of the Guildry Incorporation of Dundee' was held in the Guild Hall, to discuss the 'petitioning of Parliament … for the reconstruction of the Tay Bridge'[80] and the papers were asking how quickly it could be started. It was finally opened on 20 June 1887. It stood and still stands within sight of the ruins of the first Tay Bridge, whose broken stumps are a constant reminder of the human tragedy.

On 29 December 1879, the day after the accident, *The Annual Register* commented, 'No conclusive evidence could be produced to show whether the train was blown off the rails and so dragged the girders down, or whether the bridge was blown away and the train ran into the chasm thus made.'

So, do we know now what they didn't know then? The answer is – not for sure. The same questions are still being asked and the answers are still as probable as they ever were. One only has to read the chapter 'Hindsight' in Peter Lewis' book to see that this is the case, despite the fact that 'engineering skills and methods have changed almost beyond recognition'. So, presumably, has the knowledge. We do know that Victorian engineers and bridge builders learnt enough from the mistakes to change things. As Lewis also says, 'There is no doubt that the disaster marked a turning point in the way bridges were designed, built and managed', and we do know that recommendations were carried out and new standards set. We also know that, whilst these passengers (whatever the number might be) died 'unnecessarily'[81] because of the abject failure of others, their deaths resulted in a better level of safety for future railway travellers. Knowing that, however, will never be enough.

NOTES

Introduction

1   Having said that I bear in mind the horror of the recent
    Underground bombings and railway accidents
2   Cox, Hayter F., *The Oldest Accident Office in the World*, 1949
3   www.aviva.com/about-us/heritage
4   *Aberdeen Weekly Journal*, 9 January 1880
5   Smiles, Samuel, *The Life of George Stephenson and his son Robert
    Stephenson*
6   *Illustrated London News*, 24 September 1887
7   *Great Western Railway Magazine*, Vol.4, p. 137
8   His words
9   HC Deb, 8 May 1888, Vol. 325, cc. 1667–707. Mr Channing, MP
    (Northampton, E.)
10 *Manchester Courier* and *Lancashire General Advertiser*, Saturday
    4 January 1890
11 Page, Herbert W., *Railway Injuries in their Medico-legal and Clinical
    Aspects*, Charles Griffin & Co., 1891
12 *The Railway Magazine*, Vol. 1. July–December 1897

Chapter 1

1   As described by the *Observer*, 19 September 1830

2   *Liverpool Mercury*, Friday 17 September 1830
3   *Staffordshire Advertiser*, Saturday 18 September 1830
4   'A Railer' was the pseudonym for the writer of the article, 'The
      Opening of the Liverpool and Manchester Railroad', *Blackwood's
      Edinburgh Magazine*, September 1830
5   Ibid.
6   Simon Garfield, as quoted in *The Guardian*, 19 October 2002
7   Charles Greville was an aristocrat who became one of the finest
      political diarists of his day. His diaries are generally known as
      The Greville Papers. These quotes were written three days after
      Huskisson's death
8   Oh but that he had paid attention
9   Gore's *Liverpool General Advertiser*
10   *Mersey Times* website
11   Charles Greville
12   www.resco.co.uk/history
13   *Creevey Papers*, Thomas Creevey, 19 September 1830
14   Samuel Smiles 1899
15   Gore's *Liverpool General Advertiser*
16   Fanny Kemble
17   My italics for emphasis.
18   His words in a letter to Mrs Gaskell
19   Brougham, writing to Macvey Napier, 16 September 1830.
      Selections from the correspondence of the late Macvey Napier, 1879
20   Samuel Smiles, 1899
21   Henry Booth was the L&M Railway Company secretary and
      treasurer, *Account of the Liverpool and Manchester Railway*, 1830

Chapter 2

1   Bourne, *Great Western Railway*, David & Charles Reprints, 1970
2   Ibid.
3   Simmons, J., *The Railways of Britain: A Journey through History*,
      Macmillan, 1986
4   *Bristol Mercury*, 1 January 1842
5   I am sure MacDermott didn't mean this to sound insensitive
6   *The Times*, 25 December 1841
7   *The Railway Gazette*, August 1940
8   *The Mechanics Magazine*, 1 January 1842

9   *Bristol Mercury*, 1 January 1842

10   *Western Times*, 1 January 1842

11   *The Essex Standard and General Advertiser for the Eastern Counties*, Friday 31 December 1841

12   Nock, O.S., *The Railways of Britain*, 1951

13   *Chelmsford Chronicle*, Friday 31 December 1861

14   Ibid.

15   Andrews, Cyril Bruyn, *The Railway Age*, Country Life Ltd, 1937

16   *The Times*, 9 September 1841

17   *North Devon Journal*, 30 December 1841

18   Gray, Adrian, 'A Review of Transport and the Law of Deodand', www.rchs.org.uk/trial/J212_26LawofDeodand

19   Ibid.

20   *The Railway Gazette*, 9 August 1940

21   www.railway archive.co.uk BoT_Sonning1842

Chapter 3

1   These two were not to be amongst those who eventually established the company

2   John Clarke's book, *The Brookwood Necropolis Railway*, informs and provides most of the facts relating to the writing on this subject (unless otherwise stated)

3   *Carlisle Journal*, Saturday 23 October 1841

4   Clarke, J., 2006

5   Ibid.

6   See Clarke, J., 2006, for the very interesting details of this

7   As quoted in a report by William Moorsom, the LNC's first Engineer, in Clarke, J., 2006

8   Clarke, J., 2006

Chapter 4

1   Simmons, J., *The Victorian Railway*, Thames and Hudson, 1995

2   Williams, Frederick, *History of the Midland Railway: Its Rise and Progress*, Strahan & Co., 1888

3   Ibid.

4   Including the station and the especially the Grand Hotel, which was not designed by Barlow

5   See also section of The Tay Bridge Disaster

6   Barlow received considerable help and advice on this from
     Rowland Mason Ordish, another outstanding Victorian engineer
     whose works include the Albert Bridge, Chelsea, and the Royal
     Albert Hall

7   'Agar Town and the Midland Railway', *Old and New London*,
     Vol. 5, 1878, pp. 368–73, http://www.british-history.ac.uk/report.
     aspx?compid=45243

8   Trachtenberg, M. and Hyman, I., 'Architecture: from Prehistory to
     Post-Modernism', H.N. Abrams, University of Minnesota, 1986

9   This power came as part of their Act of Parliament

10   George Godwin, *London Shadows*, George Routledge & Co., 1854

11   'Agar Town and the Midland Railway', *Old and New London*,
     Vol. 5, 1878, pp. 368–73, http://www.british-history.ac.uk/report.
     aspx?compid=45243

12   Swensen, Steven P., 'Mapping Poverty in Agar Town', *The Nature of
     Evidence: How Well Do 'Facts' Travel?*, London School of Economics,
     2006

13   *Lloyd's Weekly Newspaper*, November 1857. The article was regard-
     ing the prosecution of an architect and builder who were in the
     process of the disinterment of a graveyard in Camden Town in
     order to build a new school

14   Whilst published under the name of his second wife, Florence Hardy,
     it is known that the majority of the work was by Hardy himself

15   Aston, Joseph, *Metrical Records of Manchester: In which its History is
     Traced*, London, 1822

16   Reports from Commissioners: 1826–27

17   Everett, J., *Panorama of Manchester and Railway Companion*, 1834

18   Epidemics Timeline – http://www.kdfhs.org.uk

19   Love, Benjamin, *Manchester as it is*, Love and Barton, 1839

20   Marshall, 1969

21   Hardy, Florence, *The Life of Thomas Hardy*, Macmillan, 1962

22   'Agar Town and the Midland Railway', *Old and New London*, Vol. 5,
     1878, from British History Online

23   *New York Times*, Friday 8 June 1860

24   *The Morning Post*, October 1860

25   See section on Brookwood Cemetery

26   Clarke and the R&CHS

27   Clarke, J., 2006

28 'Farringdon Road', *Survey of London*, Vol. 46, South and East Clerkenwell, pp. 358–84, 2008, http://www.british-history.ac.uk/report.aspx?compid=119427

Chapter 5

1   Although this was not the case for its use in warfare, and it is said that it was the realisation that his name would always be linked to war, death and carnage that prompted Nobel to leave his money to help promote peace

2   August Spies, the editor of an anarchist newspaper in Chicago, in 1886, put it into words, 'A pound of dynamite is worth a bushel of bullets', 'The Anarchists: For Jihadist Read Anarchist', *Economist*, 18 August 2005

3   Andrews, Cyril Bruyn, 1937

4   'Farringdon Road', *Survey of London*, Vol. 46, South and East Clerkenwell, pp. 358–84, 2008, http://www.british-history.ac.uk/report.aspx?compid=119427

5   Bennett, Alfred Rosling, *London and Londoners in the Eighteen-fifties and Sixties*, 1924, http://www.victorianlondon.org

6   *St James's Gazette*, 16 February 1894: 3 – 'Words and Deeds' cited in *The Conradian*

7   'The Anarchists: For Jihadist Read Anarchist', *Economist*, 18 August 2005

8   Hoffman, Bruce, 'Terrorism in History: Terrorism's Tactical Resonance: The Fenian Dynamiters', *Journal of Conflict Studies*, Winter 2007

9   *Irish World*, 4 December 1875 (New York), quoted in Kenna, Shane, 'The Fenian Dynamite Campaign and the Irish American Impetus for Dynamite Terror 1881–1885', *Student Pulse* – Online Student Academic Journal, Vol. 3, No. 12, 2011

10 Hoffman, Bruce, 2007

11 Kenna, Shane, 'The Fenian Dynamite Campaign and the Irish American Impetus for Dynamite Terror 1881–1885', *Student Pulse* – Online Student Academic Journal, Vol. 3, No. 12, 2011

12 Ibid.

13 Ibid.

14 *Leeds Times*, 14 April 1883

15 *The Times*, headline

16   L&NWR Journal
17   *The Times*, 14 September 1880
18   L&NWR Journal, as taken from *Illustrated London News*,
     25 September 1880
19   *Illustrated Police News*, Saturday 18 September 1880
20   Ibid.
21   *Bristol Mercury*, Thursday 16 September 1880
22   Mary Forsyth, L&NWR Journal
23   *The Times*, Wednesday 15 September 1880
24   Whitbread, J.R., *The Railway Policeman*, Harrap & Co., 1961
25   Neele, G.P., *Railway Reminiscences*, McCorquodale & Co. Ltd, 1904
26   Ibid.
27   Ibid.
28   *The Times*, 16 September 1880
29   Ibid.
30   *The Times*, 29 September 1880
31   My italics for emphasis
32   Norman Pattenden, in L&NWR Journal, quoting Neele
33   http://www.btp.police.uk
34   *Dundee Courier*, 11 December 1883
35   *The Morning Post*, 1 November 1883
36   *The Freeman's Journal*, 11 December 1883
37   *Illustrated Police News/The Standard*, 1 November 1883
38   Ibid.
39   *Dundee Courier & Argus*, 1 November 1883
40   *Freeman's Journal*, 1 November 1883
41   *The Standard*, 1 November 1883
42   *The York Herald*, 1 November 1883
43   *Freeman's Journal*, December 1883 and *Dundee Courier*, Tuesday
     11 December 1883
44   *Sheffield Daily Telegraph*, 11 December 1883
45   *Lloyd's Weekly Newspaper*, 4 November 1883
46   *Shields Daily Gazette*, 8 November 1883
47   *Pall Mall Gazette*, 26 February 1884
48   *The Times*, 26 February
49   *The Times*, 27 February
50   Ibid.
51   Ibid.
52   Ibid.

53   'Spear break van' obviously refers to a van with a 'brake' system for
     the guard to operate. What is intriguing here, is why it has its own
     particular name as against the normal 'brake van'. Alan M. Levitt
     (New York) of the R&CHS says, 'the term "spear break van" (or
     a variation of it) appears ten times in the transcript of the trial ...
     from the context it can be deduced that there were "regular" break
     van vehicles in use. In addition, there were '"break compartments"
     in third-class carriages. The latter were considered as "spear" or
     extra – available for use when it was less convenient to use the
     "regular break vans". To peek at the word formation, *break* evolved
     into *brake* by the reformation of *ea* into *a*, and adding a final *e* to
     the root. Reforming the *ea* of *spear* into *a* and adding a final *e* to
     the root, one has *spare*'

54   *The Times*, 3 January 1885

55   http://oldbaileyonline.org – Tim Hitchcock, Robert Shoemaker,
     Clive Emsley, Sharon Howard and Jamie McLaughlin, *et al.*, *The
     Old Bailey Proceedings Online, 1674–1913*

56   *The Bath Chronicle*, 21 May 1885

57   Burgoyne, Mary, 'Conrad among the Anarchists: Documents
     on Martial Bourdin and the Greenwich Bombing' in Allan H.
     Simmons and J.H. Stape (ed.) *The Secret Agent: Centennial Essays*,
     2007, pp.147–85, quoting *St James's Gazette*, 16 February 1894

58   Ibid.

59   In 1901 he can be found on Pankhurst Prison records

60   http://www.thefullwiki.org/aldersgatestreet. The station's name
     was shortened to Aldersgate in 1910, then changed to Aldersgate
     and Barbican in 1923 and finally, to its present day name Barbican
     in 1968

61   *Matatura Ensign*, Issue 303, 1 July 1897, New Zealand

62   *Lloyd's Weekly Newspaper*, 2 May 1897

63   Ibid.

64   *Matatura Ensign*, Issue 303, 1 July 1897, New Zealand

65   *Lloyd's Weekly Newspaper*, 2 May 1897

66   *Hartlepool Mail*, 27 April 1897

67   *The Times*, 26 April 1897

68   *The Times*, 26 April 1897, and *Lloyd's Weekly Newspaper*, 2 May 1897

69   *The Times*, 26 April 1897

70   *The Times*, 25 May 1897

71   *Illustrated Police News*, 5 June 1897

72   *Morning Post*, 25 May 1897

73   Ibid.

74   *The Times*, 25 May 1897

75   *Lloyd's Weekly Newspaper*, 2 May 1897

Chapter 6

1   Tolson, J. and Vamplew, W., 'Derailed: Railways and Horse-racing
     Revisited', *The Sports Historian*, Vol. 18 (2), November 1998,
     pp. 34–49

2   As stated in Railway Inspector Major Marindin's report to the
     Board of Trade.

3   Jenkinson, David, 'The end of an era, 1901–22', *British Railway
     Carriages of the 20th Century*, Vol. 1, Guild Publishing, 1988, p. 10

4   The Midland Railway was no stranger to 'excursion' accidents,
     having already experienced Long Eaton on 9 October 1869, and
     Kildwick on 27 August 1875

5   Sunday 25 September 1887

6   *Hampshire Advertiser*, Wednesday 21 September 1887

7   *Sheffield Daily Telegraph*, Thursday 22 September 1887

8   *Leeds Mercury*, Monday 19 September, 1887

9   *London Standard*, Monday 19 September 1887

10   Herbert Page, in Thorburn, 'A Contribution to the Surgery of the
     Spinal Cord', 1889, p. 69

11   *Hull Daily Mail*, Monday 26 September 1887

12   Ibid.

13   *Sheffield Independent*, Friday 30 September

14   *Shields Daily Gazette*, Wednesday 5 October 1887

15   *Hull Daily Mail*, Wednesday 5 October 1887

16   *Sheffield Independent*, Saturday 2 June 1888

17   Ibid.

18   *The Times*, 4 June 1888

19   *Sheffield Independent*, Tuesday 20 December 1887

20   *The Standard*, Friday 30 December 1887

21   Ibid.

22   *The Standard*

23   *Sunderland Daily Echo and Shipping Gazette*, Wednesday 17 October
     1888

24   *Sheffield Independent*, Friday 7 June 1889

25   Report to the Board of Trade

26   *Dundee Courier*, Friday 23 September 1887

27   *The Locomotive Journal*, Vol. 83, ASLEF

28   Ibid.

29   Nock, O.S., *Historic Railway Disasters*, Ian Allen Ltd, 1987, p. 11

30   Kidner, *A Short History of the Railway Carriage*, The Oakwood Press

31   See 'The Newark Brake Trials and After' (Part 1 & 2) by Jeffrey
     Wells, *Backtrack*, Vol. 13, No. 2, February 1999, for an explanation

32   It was not until after the appalling accident of Armagh in Ireland
     in 1889, when 80 died and some 262 were injured, that the 1889
     Regulation of Railways Act made automatic continuous brakes on
     all passenger trains compulsory

33   Nock, O.S., 1987, p. 49

34   Peter Witt, R&CHS

35   *Manchester Times*, Saturday 19 November 1887

Chapter 7

1   *Pall Mall Gazette*, 3 August 1880

2   *The British Architect*, 2 January 1880, p. 9

3   Grothe, A., 'The Tay Bridge', *Good Words* magazine, 1878, p. 103

4   Over the 'high girder' section, the girders were 14ft 10in apart
     (centre to centre), immediately adjacent to the high girder sec-
     tion the remaining girders, where the track was laid on top of
     the girder, were of the same width, but they narrowed nearer the
     shore, to as little as 9ft apart. Allan Rodgers, North British Railway
     Study Group

5   Swinfen, David, *The Fall of the Tay Bridge*, Mercat Press, Edinburgh,
     1994

6   Dow, 'The Tay Bridge Letters' (unpublished) research based on the
     original letters held at the Scottish Record Office, Edinburgh

7   Dow, 'The Tay Bridge Letters' (unpublished)

8   North British Railway Study Group

9   Lewis, 2005

10   Swinfen, quoting the *Dundee Advertiser*, 26 September 1871

11   Grothe, 1878, p. 103

12   Reynolds, M., *Engine-Driving Life – Stirring Adventures and Incidents
     in the Lives of Locomotive Engine-Drivers*, 1882. Reprint, Hugh
     Evelyn, 1968

13 Gren, Andre, *The Bridge is Down! Dramatic Eyewitness Accounts of the Tay Bridge Disaster, 28 December 1879*, Silver Link Publishing Ltd, 2008

14 Rothery Report

15 Cattanach of North British Railway Study Group

16 This is debateable

17 *Aberdeen Journal*, Wednesday 31 December 1879

18 Nicoll et al., *Victims of the Tay Rail Bridge Disaster*, 2005

19 Several witnesses gave evidence of what they had seen

20 Rothery Report

21 Prebble, John, *The High Girders: The Story of the Tay Bridge Disaster*, Book Club Associates, 1975

22 *Daily Gazette*, Monday 29 December 1879

23 *Aberdeen Weekly Journal*, 9 January 1880

24 *Birmingham Daily Post*, Tuesday 30 December 1879

25 *North British Railway Study Group Journal*, No. 107, December 2009, p. 10

26 Reynolds, M., *Engine-Driving Life – Stirring Adventures and Incidents in the Lives of Locomotive Engine-Drivers*, 1882. Reprint, Hugh Evelyn, 1968

27 Cameron, *NBRSG Journal*, No. 107

28 Cameron

29 *Manchester Courier and Lancashire General Advertiser*, Thursday 1 January 1880

30 Rodgers, *NBRSG Journal*, No. 107

31 Prebble, 1975

32 Rothery Report

33 Henry Law's Report

34 Spencer, Alfred, *Life of Harry Watts – Sixty Years Sailor and Diver*, Hills & Co., 1911

35 Nicoll et al., 2005

36 Prebble, 1975

37 Ibid.

38 *Dundee Courier*, Tuesday 13 April 1880

39 *Aberdeen Journal*, 8 January 1880

40 Ibid.

41 Ibid.

42 Nicoll et al., 2005

43 *Glasgow Herald*, 9 January 1880

44 *Aberdeen Journal*, 8 January 1880

45 Nicoll et al., 2005

46 *Aberdeen Journal*, 8 January 1880

47 Ibid.

48 Nicoll et al., 2005

49 *Daily Birmingham Post*, 30 December 1879

50 *The Times*, 30 December 1879; *Alnwick Mercury*, 3 January 1880; and *Birmingham Post*, 30 December 1879

51 Nicoll's research

52 *Aberdeen Journal*, 31 December 1879

53 *Aberdeen Journal*, 15 January 1880

54 *Dundee Courier*, 10 February 1880

55 Ibid.

56 Nicoll et al., 2005

57 *Dundee Courier*, 10 February 1880

58 *The Star,* 7 February 1880; *Nottingham Evening Post* and *Dundee Courier*, 10 February 1880

59 *Aberdeen Journal*, 8 January 1880

60 *Aberdeen Journal*, 8 January 1880

61 Reynolds, M., *Engine-Driving Life – Stirring Adventures and Incidents in the Lives of Locomotive Engine-Drivers*, 1882. Reprint, Hugh Evelyn, 1968

62 Mitchell's other two children, D.M. Jr and Andrew, married and raised families of their own. They are buried in Edinburgh and Glasgow respectively

63 Reynolds, 1968

64 Swinfen, 1994

65 Nicoll et al., 2005

66 *Staffordshire Sentinel*, 8 January 1880

67 Prebble, 1975

68 *The Times*, 30 December 1879

69 30 December 1879

70 See Tay Bridge Memorial Fund Group site, http://www.tay-bridgememorial.co.uk

71 Nicoll's research

72 *Scotland's People* website, http://www.scotlandspeople.gov.uk

73 Rothery's Report

74 Lewis, 2008

75 Rothery's Report

76   Swinfen, 1994, p. 80
77   *The Times*, Thursday 15 July 1880
78   About £13,000 today, using an RPI convertor
79   Cattanach, unpublished manuscript
80   Dow, 'The Tay Bridge Letters'
81   Lewis, p. 170

BIBLIOGRAPHY

Books

Andrews, Cyril Bruyn, *The Railway Age*, Country Life Ltd, 1937

Aston, Joseph, *Metrical Records of Manchester: In which its History is Traced*, 1822

Aston, Joseph, *A Picture of Manchester*, 1826

Axon, William E.A. (ed.), *The Annals of Manchester: A Chronological Record from the Earliest Times to the End of 1885*, Heywood, Deansgsate and Ridgefield, 1886

Barnes, Eric G., *The Rise of the Midland Railway 1844–1874*, George Allen & Unwin Ltd, 1966

Bennett, Alfred Rosling, *London and Londoners in the Eighteen-Fifties and Sixties*, T. Fisher Unwin Ltd, 1924

Biddle, Gordon, *Victorian Stations*, David & Charles, 1973

Billson, Peter, *Derby and the Midland Railway*, The Breedon Books Publishing Company, 1996

Booth, Henry, *Account of the Liverpool and Manchester Railway*, Liverpool, Wales and Barnes, 1830

Bourne, John C., *A Reproduction of the History and Description of the Great Western Railway from Drawings taken expressly for this Work and Executed in Lithography*, David & Charles Reprints, 1970

Brandon, David and Brooke, Alan, *Blood on the Tracks – A History of Railway Crime in Britain*, The History Press, 2009

Briggs, Asa, *A Social History of England*, Weidenfeld and Nicholson, 1994

British Railway Disasters, Ian Allen Publishing, Fourth Impression, 2007

Butterworth, Alex, *The World That Never Was: A True Story of Dreamers, Schemers, Anarchists and Secret Agents*, The Bodley Head, 2010

Clarke, John M., *The Brookwood Necroplis Railway*, The Oakwood Press, 4th edition, 2006

Course, Edwin, *London Railways*, B.T. Batsford Ltd, 1962

Cox, Hayter F., *The Oldest Accident Office in the World, being the Study of the Railway Passengers' Assurance Company Centenary 1849–1949*, 1949

Ellis, Hamilton, *The Pictorial Encyclopaedia of Railways*, Hamlyn, 6th Impression, 1974

Engels, Frederick, *The Condition of the Working Class in England in 1844: with a Preface Written in 1892*

Everett, J., *Panorama of Manchester, and Railway Companion*, 1834

Ferneyhough, Frank, *Liverpool & Manchester Railway 1830–1980*, Robert Hale, 1980

Foxell, Clive, *Images of 150 Years of the Metropolitan Railway*, The History Press, 2013

Freeman, Michael, *Railways and the Victorian Imagination*, Yale University Press, 1999

Gibbs, Ken, *The Steam Locomotive: An Engineering History*, Amberley Publishing, 2012

Godwin, George, FRS, *London Shadows: A Glance at the 'Homes' of the Thousands*, George Routledge & Co., 1854

Gren, Andre, *The Bridge is Down! Dramatic eyewitness accounts of the Tay Bridge disaster 28 December 1879*, Silver Link Publishing Ltd, 2008

Hardy, Florence Emily, *The Life of Thomas Hardy*, Macmillan, 1962

Hobsbawm, E.J., *Industry and Empire*, Pelican, 1969

Kellett, John R., *The Impact of Railways on Victorian Cities*, Routledge & Kegan Paul, 1969

Kidner, R.W., *A Short History of Mechanical Traction and Travel*, Part 5 – 'A Short History of the Railway Carriage', The Oakwood Press, 1946

Love, Benjamin, *Manchester As It Is*, Love and Barton, 1839

MacDermott, E.T., *History of the Great Western Railway*, Vols 1 & 2, Great Western Railway Company, 1927

Maxwell, Sir Herbert (ed.), *The Creevey Papers: A Selection from the Correspondence & Diaries of the Late Thomas Creevey M P. Born 1768 Died 1838*, John Murray, 1904

Napier, Macvey, *Selections from the Correspondence of the Late Macvey Napier*, 1879 (archive.org)

Neele, George P., *Railway Reminiscences*, McCorquodale & Co. Ltd, 1904

Nock, O.S., *British Trains: Past and Present*, B.T. Batsford Ltd, 1951

Nock, O.S., *Historic Railway Disasters*, Ian Allen Ltd, 4th Edition, 1987

Page, Herbert W., *Railway Injuries in their Medico-legal and Clinical Aspects*, Charles Griffin & Co., 1891

Page, Norman, *Oxford Reader's Companion to Hardy*, Oxford University Press, 2000

Perkin, Harold, *The Age of the Railway*, David and Charles, 1971

Peters, William, *Railway Dangers and how to Avoid them*, Effingham Wilson, 1853

Prebble, John, *The High Girders: The Story of the Tay Bridge Disaster*, Book Club Associates, 1975

Raynes, John R., *Engines and Men: The History of the Associated Society of Locomotive Engineers and Firemen*, Goodall & Suddick Ltd, 1916 (openlibrary.org)

Reports from Commissioners (seven volumes – Charities in England and Wales; Counties of Gloucester, Lancaster, Middlesex; Southampton; Surrey; York), Session 21, November 1826–2 July 1827, Vol. 9, p. 114 (Google books)

Reynolds, Michael, *Engine-Driving Life – Stirring Adventures and Incidents in the Lives of Locomotive Engine-Drivers*, 1882. Reprint, Hugh Evelyn, 1968

Richards, Jeffrey and Mackenzie, John, *The Railway Station: A Social History*, Oxford University Press, 1988

Rolt, L.T.C., *Red for Danger*, Sutton Publishing, 1998

Simmons, Allan H. and Stape, J.H. (ed.), *The Secret Agent: Centennial Essays*, The Conradian, 2007

Simmons, Jack, *The Railways of Britain: A Journey Through History*, Macmillan, 1986

Simmons, Jack, *The Victorian Railway*, Thames and Hudson, 1995

Smiles, Samuel, 'The Locomotive: George and Robert Stephenson', in *Lives of the Engineers*, Vol. 5, John Murray, 1879

Spencer, Alfred, *Life of Harry Watts – Sixty Years Sailor and Diver*, Hills & Co., 1911 (Open Library)

Swinfen, David, *The Fall of the Tay Bridge*, Mercat Press, 1994

Whitbread, J.R., *The Railway Policeman*, Harrap & Co., 1961

Wilson, H. Raynar, *Railway Accidents: Legislation and Statistics 1825–1924*, The Raynar Wilson Company, 1925

Williams, Frederick S., *Williams's Midland Railway: Its Rise and Progress*, 1876. Reprint, David & Charles Ltd, 1968

All Stations: A Journey through 150 Years of Railway History, Thames and Hudson, 1981

Articles

Greville, Charles, *Charles Greville Papers*, Project Gutenberg.

Grothe, A., 'The Tay Bridge', in two parts, from Donald Macleod (ed.), *Good Words*, 1878

Hoffman, Bruce, 'Terrorism in History', *Journal of Conflict Studies*, Winter 2007

Kenna, Shane, 'The Fenian Dynamite Campaign and the Irish American Impetus for Dynamite Terror 1881–1885', Student Pulse – Online Student Academic Journal, Vol. 3, No. 12, 2011

Kenna, Shane, 'Irish History – The Irish Story – One Skilled Scientist is Worth an Army – The Fenian Dynamite Campaign 1881–85'

Lewis, Peter R. and Reynolds, Ken, 'Forensic Engineering: a reappraisal of the Tay Bridge Disaster', *Interdisciplinary Science Reviews*, Vol. 27, No 4, 2002

Lewis, Peter R. and Gagg, Colin, 'Aesthetics versus function: the fall of the Dee Bridge, 1847', *Interdisciplinary Science Reviews*, Vol. 29, No. 2, 2004

Martin, T. and Macleod I.A., 'The Tay Rail Bridge Disaster: a reappraisal based on modern analysis methods', Inst. Civil Engineers, Paper 10668, 1995

Pantony, M.F., 'Hazards XVI: Analysing the Past: Planning the Future', Symposium Institute of Chemical Engineers, UMI, 2001

Pinsdorf, Marion K., 'Engineering Dreams into Disaster: History of the Tay Bridge', *Business and Economic History*, Vol. 26, No. 2, Winter 1997

Swensen, Steven P. 'Mapping Poverty in Agar Town: Economic Conditions Prior to the Development of St Pancras Station in 1866', in *The Nature of Evidence: How Well Do 'Facts' Travel*, London School of Economics: Department of Economic History, 2006

Tolson, J. and Vamplew, W., 'Derailed: Railways and Horse-Racing Revisited', *The Sports Historian*, Vol. 18, November 1998

Trachtenberg, Marvin and Hyman, Isabelle, 'Architecture: From Prehistory to Post-Modernism – the Western Tradition', H.N. Abrams, University of Minnesota, 1986

Wells, Jeffrey, 'The Newark Brake Trials and After', *Backtrack*, Vol. 13, No. 2, February 1999

Journals

London & North Western Railway Society Journal – ISSN 1352-2833
T839 Forensic Engineering, Resource C, The Open University
T839 Forensic Engineering, Block 3 – 'Catastrophic failures', Peter Lewis and Dai Jones, with the assistance of Ken Reynolds and Addison Bain. The Open University
'The Tay Bridge Disaster 130th Anniversary Special' (Journal 107), North British Railway Study Group, December 2009

Newspapers and Magazines

Aberdeen Journal
Alnwick Journal
Barrows Worcester Journal
Birmingham Daily Post
Bristol Mercury
Chelmsford Chronicle
Daily Birmingham Post
Daily Gazette for Middlesborough
Dundee Advertiser
Glasgow Herald
Hartlepool Mail
Huddersfield Daily Chronicle
Leeds Mercury
Leicester Chronicle and Leicester Mercury
Liverpool Advertiser
Lloyd's Weekly
Morning Post
Manchester Courier and Lancashire General Advertiser
Manchester Times
North Devon Journal
Northern-Eastern Daily Gazette
Northampton Mercury
Observer

Reynold's Newspaper
Saturday Review
Shields Daily Gazette
Staffordshire Sentinel
The British Architect
The Daily Gazette
The Daily Post
The Dublin Evening Mail
The Era
The Essex Standard and General Advertiser for the Eastern Counties
The Examiner
The Great Western Railway Magazine
The Louth and North Lincolnshire Advertiser
The Morning Post
The Railway Magazine
The Saturday Review
The Sheffield Local Register
The Standard
The Times

Websites

http://www.aviva.com/about-us

http://www.british-history.ac.uk/report.aspx?compid=45243 – 'Agar Town and the Midland Railway', *Old and New London*, Vol. 5, 1878, pp. 368–73

http://www.btp.police.uk/about_us/our_history/timeline/time-line_1851–1950

http://www.culture24.org.uk – 'From Anarchist to Islamist – A History of Terrorism in London', Kate Smith, September 2009

http://www.engineeringtimelines.com

http://www.theirishstory.com/2012/02/13/one-skilled-scientist-is-worth-an-army-the-fenian-dynamite-campaign-1881-85/#.UtQLhGRdUhw

http://www.leisureandculturedundee.com

http://www.london-se1.co.uk/news/view/6067

http://www.mtholyoke.edu/courses/rschwart/ind_rev/index.html – the Industrial Revolution & The Railway System http://www.oldbaileyonline.org – version 7.0, Tim Hitchcock, Robert Shoemaker, Clive Emsley, Sharon Howard and Jamie McLaughlin, et al., The Old Bailey Proceedings Online, 1674–1913

httt://www.railwaymapsanddocuments.com

http://www.railwaysarchive.co.uk – accident returns

http://www.rchs.org.uk/trial/J212_26LawofDeodand – Adrian Gray, 'A Review of Transport and the Law of Deodand'

http://www.taybridgememorial.co.uk

http://www.timetravel-britain.com

http://www.thenewyorktimes/1860/07

http://www.victorianlondon.org-publication

http://www.victoriantimes.cdlr.strath.ac.uk

INDEX